PERCEPTUAL-MOTOR LESSON PLANS LEVEL-1

8th Edition

D1478068

Basic and *Practical* Lesson Plans
for
Perceptual-Motor Programs in Preschool
and the
Elementary Grades

Level-1 Covers Preschool and Kindergarten to First Grade

Editor
Frank Alexander

by
Jack Capon

Text Artist
John Lewis

Level-1 Lessons-- *Page 1* ------------------------------------*25 Week Program*

36,000 Books in Print as of 2004

Previously copyrighted in 1975 by Jack Capon
Copyright © 1998 Jack Capon

(8th Edition)

I SBN 0-915256-03-7

Published
by
FRONT ROW EXPERIENCE
540 Discovery Bay Blvd.
Discovery Bay, CA 94514-9454

NOTICE
The information contained in this book is true and complete to the best of our knowledge. It is offered with no
guarantees on the part of the author or Front Row Experience. The author and publisher disclaim
all liability in connection with the use of this book.

CONTENTS

Copyright © Jack Capon 1998

Overview Of Basic Perceptual-Motor Equipment ....

Equipment Construction Diagrams ....

Program Suppliers ....

Program Equipment List ....

Parent Communication Aides ....

Perception Games ....

Lessons Grouped According to Equipment and Type of Activities ....

Resources ....

ABOUT THE AUTHOR

Jack Capon was known nationally and internationally for his *practical* application of Movement Education to the classroom environment. By means of his numerous workshops that he conducted throughout the world, Jack Capon has shown how teachers and others interested in Movement Education can start their own successful programs. It's been told that the original founder of the nationwide and now worldwide chain of Gymboree fitness centers for kids got her inspiration and many of her ideas from observing Jack Capon's programs in action and in attending many of his early workshops. Likewise, Jack's fame and Movement expertise influenced the creation of another major Movement Education chain that is based in Australia called Toddler Kindy Gymbaroo. Gymbaroo is now one of the dominant children's fitness centers in Australia and is spreading into other countries. The fact that you can start a business using Jack Capon-like activities for kids is further testament to the obvious that his programs do work and give a valuable boost to the development of any child in the early childhood years. This 8th Edition Level-1 book is a further effort by Jack to provide teachers and schools with a practical approach to organizing the physical education program in the preschool to elementary grades.

Jack Capon was active in Movement Education from the early 1960's right on up to the mid 1990's when by an ironic twist of fate he was forced into early retirement by the onslaught of a rare neurological disorder called Striatonigral Degeneration. In the early stages this disorder mimics the symptoms of Parkinson's disease but later on as it kills off more and more brain cells it forces its host into paraplegic-like conditions. And finally after several years of deteriorating health, Jack passed away in the summer of 1999 soon after the publication of the newest edition to his Level-2 book. But Jack's legacy lives on and thanks to Jack's many workshops over the years and to the continuing great success of his programs, many people have been trained in the Jack Capon method and are quite skilled in advising any of those who are interested in starting, restarting, or continuing his Movement Education programs. People who have been trained in the Jack Capon method and who are willing to offer their advice and assistance are listed in the Resources section at the back of this book.

Jack Capon, besides being the author of this book, has authored numerous other Movement Education books over the years. He has been a consultant to several films and videos on Movement Education and he has produced many record/cassette/CD albums on musical Movement Education activities.

Jack Capon, who spent nearly his entire professional career as the Coordinator For Physical Education in the Alameda City School District, Alameda, California, has been appointed to many positions and given many awards and honors over the years recognizing his great achievements in Movement Education and his unselfish volunteer work in his community. From 1968 to 72 he served on the Perceptual-Motor Task Force of the American Association for Health, Physical Education, Recreation and Dance (AAHPERD). He was elected National Chairman of the Elementary Physical Education section of AAHPERD in 1972. The California Association of Health, Physical Education, Recreation, and Dance (CAHPERD) presented him with their State Honor Award in 1978. Around that time AAHPERD presented him with the City and County Director's Honor Award. In 1982 the California Association of School Administrators (ACSA) selected him as the "outstanding Administrator of the Year." He served as the volunteer Director of the Special Olympics Program for 25 years for the town of Alameda, California where he lived and worked. The local Channel 4 TV station in his area honored him in 1992 with it's annual "For Those Who Care" award. The City of Alameda, California, gave him the Citizen of the Year Award in 1993. San Jose State University's College of Applied Arts and Science, San Jose, California, gave it its Distinguished Alumni Award in 1995. And he continues to be honored posthumously by many different local and national groups. Jack Capon was not only a great Movement Educator, but a great human being as well. Although Jack is no longer here with his energy and enthusiasm for Movement Education, his Perceptual-Motor Development Programs live on and continue to provide valuable help in developing the movement coordination skills necessary for the healthy development of children everywhere.

PROGRAM OBJECTIVES

Perceptual-Motor Development refers to one's ability to receive, interpret and respond successfully to sensory information. "Perception" is the receiving or input system while "motor" refers to output or responsive movement. The environment that the student is placed into will determine the type of sensory stimuli that must be processed. In this movement program, participants receive information primarily through the visual, auditory, tactile, vestibular and kinesthetic senses. All conscious and controlled movement depends on one's ability to interpret sensory information.

Traditionally in physical education programs we have centered our attention on output or performance such as: Can the student jump the rope?; Is he or she able to run fast?; Does the ball go into the basket?; etc. In Perceptual-Motor Programs we concern ourselves first with input or reception and examine how it affects one's performance. Our awareness of a total process of development now takes on great importance. Program objectives no longer are limited to the acquisition of physical skills and fitness, but rather how can we assist the student to function more successfully in all phases of the school curriculum. Our means of accomplishing this goal is through the use of carefully planned movement experiences.

One of the major roles of the teacher in a Perceptual-Motor Program then becomes that of creating an environment which will demand total mental concentration as well as physical involvement. The student is challenged to think and then respond with purposeful controlled movements. This requires the teacher to develop and maintain a positive working climate in which students understand fully their responsibilities. It does not mean the program becomes so rigid that the fun and excitement of participating are eliminated, but rather that students are responding with a combination of their best mental and physical efforts.

Perceptual-motor abilities which should be promoted include body image, balance, spatial awareness, hand-eye and foot-eye coordination (visual-motor control), laterality, directionality, proprioception, and form discrimination. Attributes of movement such as rhythm, locomotor coordination, agility, strength, and flexibility are also developed within various aspects of the program.

PRIMARY OBJECTIVES OF THIS LEVEL-1 PROGRAM ARE AS FOLLOWS:

1) Assist each student in acquiring efficient movement.
2) Promote improved sensory functioning.
3) Development of a positive self-image.

The main areas of program concentration are in promoting improved:

1) Balance Skills (Static and Dynamic)
2) Locomotor Skills (Transport Movements)
3) Hand-Eye and Foot-Eye Coordination
4) Body and Space Awareness
5) Language skills

The need for this type of movement program in our schools is becoming widely recognized by educational leaders. Students of all ages have a right to move with confidence and control. Schools have an obligation to provide meaningful programs.

PLANNING YOUR LEVEL-1 PROGRAM

The year's Level-1 Program as presented consists of 25 weekly perceptual-motor lessons. The Program is designed as a two year reinforcement course for students beginning in either preschool or kindergarten. Students who successfully complete this Level-1 Program should move on to the Level-2 Program beginning in First or Second Grade or when the teacher feels it is appropriate. However, it is important to make sure that the children can successfully complete the Level-1 activities before moving on to Level-2.

These lessons are presented to teachers as a guide in setting up a basic Perceptual-Motor Program. Teachers will have to decide how much repetition students in their classes need on any given lesson or activity. Teachers also have the responsibility of making modifications in specific activities to insure successful participation for each student in their class.

SEQUENCING OF LESSON ACTIVITIES

One of the most difficult parts of organizing a program of this type is the sequencing of challenges so that they are appropriate developmentally as well as in terms of skill progression. The Program will continue to be evaluated and refined in future editions.

It is important to realize that for each type of station (equipment item) in the Program a basic sequence or skill progression has been developed. Some stations such as the Walking Board (Balance Beam) and Mat Stunts are included in the Lesson Plans each week while other station activities are included only once every 2 or 3 weeks. The two main factors that determine the frequency of inclusion for any one type of station activity are: 1) the predetermined need for various types of experiences; and 2) the amount of continuous reinforcement deemed necessary for the refinement of basic perceptual-motor abilities as found in an average population of preschool and elementary students. It is important to note, however, that teachers should not feel locked into the lesson sequence presented in this program. It goes without saying that individual needs vary from group to group.

For some station activities such as the Walking Boards, Mat Stunts, and Bouncer, the Challenges are reviewed in the following lesson while for other types of stations this review has not been deemed necessary due to the close similarity of the new challenges.

Teachers will find that due to the careful sequencing and organization of the stations, a high degree of success and interest will be maintained throughout the 25 weeks of programming.

SETTING UP YOUR CLASSROOM

Each week of the Lesson Plans section contains 2 lessons. Each lesson is designed to last approximately 30 minutes. A typical lesson has 3 stations. Each station is a separate perceptual-motor activity. The stations are intended to be all run at the same time within your classroom or designated perceptual-motor activity area.

Have your students begin the movement activities in the 3 stations for that lesson. Your students should be evenly divided among the stations so that you have approximately the same number of students beginning an activity station at the same time. Students at each station may be grouped either homogenous (children with similar abilities) or heterogenous (children with mixed abilities) depending on which procedure the teacher feels would best benefit the students. It is also best to have each group of students change stations at the same time. This allows for better control and organization. The teacher can determine, in relation to total lesson time available, when the groups should rotate.

In the station examples on the next page: Students who finish **Station-3** go on to **Station-1**
Students who finish **Station-1** go on to **Station-2**
Students who finish **Station-2** go on to **Station-3**

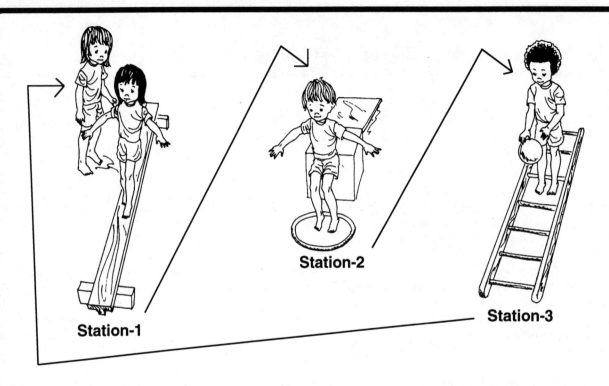

Station-1

Station-2

Station-3

Having several activity stations in each lesson allows the students to: proceed faster through all of the activities; receive individualized help; experience a wider variety of perceptual-motor movements; and...have more "fun".

INTRODUCING THE LESSON

When beginning your lesson there are two common approaches which may be used in orientating your students: 1) Review with the entire class the motor challenges or tasks which the students will engage in at each station. (This can be accomplished quickly by using a student at each station to demonstrate.); or 2) Have an aide at each station explain the activities and present verbal challenges to each group individually as they rotate to that station.

Whether the first or second approach is used strongly depends on the availability of aides at each station plus their insight and ability.

(Note that the activities for the Challenges in each station are written in the ways that you might say to your students. Feel free to phrase the Challenges any way you like. Whatever works. Text in parentheses are special notes to the teacher.)

USE OF ADDITIONAL STATIONS

Although only 3 activity or learning stations are included in each lesson, this does not necessarily mean that 3 stations are the ideal number to work with. Certainly if adequate space, equipment, and supervision are available, the teacher may desire to use additional stations within each lesson. An important factor to consider here is the number of students involved at each station. Students must be involved in order to have a successful program. An excessive amount of standing in lines and waiting turns defeats the program's purpose. In general, 4 to 6 students at each station is a good guide for class organization. Understandably, due to various limitations, this ratio is not always possible.

In organizing additional learning stations within any given lesson it is highly recommended that the teacher review activities from previous lessons giving particular attention to those experiences which it is felt are in need of stronger reinforcement.

Generally speaking, mat stunts and hand-eye coordination tasks profit most from this opportunity for review.

FACILITY NEEDS

It is of utmost importance to the overall success of the Level-1 Perceptual-Motor Program that an indoor facility be available for storage of equipment and conducting the program. An empty classroom or multipurpose room will provide adequate space. Upon entering the room to participate, students are asked to remove their shoes and socks. This is done for safety and to provide a better tactile and kinesthetic "feel" for movement as the student interacts with various pieces of equipment.

Of course, because of a shortage of classroom space or other restrictions, it may not be possible to have a "dedicated" facility for the Level-1 Program. And to get some ideas about an alternative method, see the section entitled, **Lessons Grouped According to Equipment and Type of Activities**, on page 212.

EQUIPMENT

Program equipment plays an important role in helping to develop motor skills. Equipment serves as a catalyst for movement and helps make the program challenging and exciting. However, there is no magic in equipment. The magic is in the student, and is brought out in the human interaction between teacher and student. Students need guidance in the correct use of equipment, and they need equipment which is appropriate to their size, strength, and coordination. The more equipment available, the more involvement of students, and hopefully, a greater opportunity for learning.

All of the 20 or so different pieces of equipment used in this Program have bee carefully selected and designed according to motor development needs of your students. There is a definite purpose and reason for every challenge used in conjunction with each piece of equipment.

It should be noted that three different levels are incorporated into the walking board challenges. The recommended *low* level is 7" high, the *intermediate* level is 11" to 13 1/2" high, and the *high* level is 19 1/2" to 20 1/2" high. After the first few weeks of lessons a new task is always introduced at the low level and then is reviewed at a higher level, either *intermediate* or *high*, in the following weeks. For more information on the needs and characteristics of Program equipment, see the sections entitled: *Overview Of Basic Perceptual-Motor Equipment, Equipment Construction Diagrams, Program Suppliers,* and *Program Equipment List.*

USE OF AIDES

The use of volunteer aides or upper grade level students to assist teachers in conducting the Program is another vital ingredient to a successful program. The aides can save valuable teaching time by setting up equipment for lessons and then assisting students in acquiring skills at one or more stations. The use of parent aides serves a dual purpose in that the importance of perceptual-motor development can be viewed first hand and community support generated for the Program.

OVERALL PROGRAMMING

The perceptual-motor program is the individualized phase of the weekly physical education program. These lessons should be reinforced with such large group experiences as rhythm activities, games, playground apparatus stunts, and movement exploration using balls, ropes, hoops, etc. It is especially important to provide additional opportunities to work with balls beyond what is included within the lesson plans in this book.

A typical overall weekly plan is presented below as an example of the type of planning necessary for a complete program:

Monday	=	Ball Skill Activity
Tuesday	=	Perceptual-Motor, Lesson #1
Wednesday	=	Game Activity
Thursday	=	Perceptual-Motor, Lesson #2
Friday	=	Rhythm Activity

SCREENING

All participants should be screened at the beginning of the program using the *Level-1 Perceptual-Motor Evaluation Scale* as given in this book. This assessment tool includes testing for a variety of perceptual-motor abilities among which are: balance, body image, spatial awareness, locomotor control, and hand-eye coordination. The results of this initial screening should be used to assess individual needs and assist the teacher in grouping students for successful program participation.

PERCEPTUAL-MOTOR TERMINOLOGY

The following terms are used in the book's lesson plans and help you accurately assess your students in the *Level-1 Perceptual-Motor Evaluation Scale*.

BODY IMAGE
The individual's concept of his or her body and its parts. The concept involves the knowledge of: a) the physical structure of the body and its parts; b) the movements and functions of the body and its parts; and c) the position of the body and its parts in relation to each other and to other objects. It forms a base for acquiring an adequate self concept.

BALANCE
The ability to assume and maintain any body position against the force of gravity. Maintenance of balance results from the interaction of the muscles working to keep the body on its base.

VISUAL-MOTOR CONTROL
Refers to the ability to successfully integrate visual and motor responses into a physical action. It enables an individual to control movement, and move easily and smoothly from place to place.

COORDINATION
The ability of the body to integrate the action of the muscles of the body to accomplish a specific movement or a series of skilled movements in the most efficient manner.

PROPRIOCEPTION
The awareness of muscular movement and position of the body in space.

GROSS-MOTOR COORDINATION
Results from the development of the skeletal or large muscles to produce efficient total body movement.

FINE-MOTOR COORDINATION
The coordinated use of small muscles resulting from the development of the muscles to the degree that they can perform specific small movements such as cutting, writing, grasping, and so on.

SUSTAINED MOVEMENTS
Motor skills executed consecutively for a number of times or continued for an interval of time.

SPACE AWARENESS (SPATIAL ORIENTATION)
Involves the ability to select a reference point to stabilize functions and to organize objects into correct perspective. It involves knowledge of the body and its position, as well as the positions of other people and objects in relation to one's body in space. Closely associated with *Body Image*.

LATERALITY
Internalizing the awareness of the difference between right and left and the ability to control the two sides of the body together or separately. Bilateral movements involve the use of both sides of the body in a simultaneous and parallel fashion as in catching a ball with two hands. Unilateral movements involve the use of one side of the body or one limb on that body side as in bouncing

a ball with one hand. Cross-laterality is the simultaneous use of different limbs on opposite sides of the body as in walking where arms and legs move in opposition to each other.

DIRECTIONALITY
Often confused with laterality. An awareness of external space outside of the body and involves: a) knowledge of directions in relation to right and left, in and out, and up and down, etc.; and b) the projection of one's self in space.

HAND-EYE COORDINATION
Refers to one's ability to use his or her eyes and hands together to accomplish a task.

FOOT-EYE COORDINATION
Refers to one's ability to use his or her eyes and feet together to accomplish a task.

OCULAR PURSUIT
Ability of the eyes to work together in following (tracking) a moving object or in focusing from one object to another.

KINESTHESIS
One's awareness of muscular movement and expenditure of energy during the performance of a skill.

PERCEPTUAL-MOTOR SKILLS
Those skills which indicate the interrelationships between the perceptual or sensory processes and motor activity and the ability of the individual to receive, interpret, and respond accurately to stimuli, either internal or external. Perceptual-motor learning involves all senses: seeing, hearing, touching, tasting, smelling, and moving or kinesthesis. Also known as *Sensory-Motor Skills* and/or *Psycho-Motor Skills*.

BEFORE YOU START

Don't forget to screen your students by using the *Level-1 Perceptual-Motor Evaluation Scale* or similar assessment instrument. Also, by testing your students again halfway through your program and at the end, you will be able to note the progress of your students and to help them be successful in those areas where they need improvement.

Before beginning your 25 week perceptual-motor program go over the following Checklist. The Checklist contains important reminders of things to do, to be aware of, and to watch for *before you start*.

CHECKLIST

1) Assist students with clothing problems. All participants are asked to remove shoes and socks before going to stations.

2) Explain lesson tasks to participants at assigned station.

3) Instruct students in correct technique and skill needed for successful participation.

4) Use student to "model" or demonstrate task, if necessary, for correct performance.

5) Provide physical assistance (hold hand, etc.), if needed, for emotional security and confidence, but gradually remove this "crutch".

6) Reinforce positive behavior of students by providing verbal recognition of successful performance.

7) Modify tasks where applicable for successful performance.

8) Add extra equipment whenever possible (in relation to available space) to allow greater involvement. Example: use several rebound nets or launching boards, if available, not just one.

9) If both walking boards (that is, low and intermediate) are involved in a lesson, have students perform on each board and rotate back and forth.

10) If full class is involved, think in terms of setting up a review station so that at least 4 stations are in operation.

11) Sometimes it is best to group students by motor deficiencies or strengths so that tasks can be more easily modified or adapted to individual abilities and needs.

12) At some stations students will receive many repetitions during a given lesson while at another station the repetitions will be limited. This cannot be helped due to the many different types of equipment and tasks or challenges used in the program.

13) The number of repetitions is not the key factor in learning...the quality of each trial is more important.

14) It is best to have students work at one station for a period of time (7 to 10 minutes) and then all groups rotate at the same time (on signal from the teacher) to a new station.

15) Success is the greatest motivator of all! Be aware of each student's ability level and make necessary task adjustments (that is, lower cross bar, place tires closer, etc.) to insure a high degree of success.

16) Whenever time allows after students have received several repetitions in "directed or structured" tasks, challenge them to discover or find a new way of performing. This allows each student to use his own creativity and skill.

17) Remember...this is a learning program. If students are not mentally involved in terms of thinking and planning their motor responses to a given task or challenge, then results will be limited in terms of stated objectives.

18) You should enhance language development by key movement words such as: under, over, through, or walk, skip, hop, throw, bend, etc.

19 Classroom control is most important. Students must be focused on the challenges presented.

20) Above all, the program you set up should allow the students to have fun so that physical activity becomes enjoyable.

SAFETY FIRST

Safety should be constantly stressed so that both students and aides are aware of their responsibilities in this important area. Participation should not be allowed without adult supervision.

Equipment must be checked on a regular basis to insure that it is safe for use. Wood equipment especially needs to be maintained free of splinters, cracks, etc. Some equipment items such as jump boxes, incline boards, and scooter boards may be carpeted for extra safety.

Improper clothing is probably the greatest safety hazard in any perceptual-motor program. Long dresses and slippery leotards worn by girls are among the biggest clothing problems. Some types of shoes and boots can be very awkward and slippery to move in. Students are safest in their bare feet.

Before the start of your program, you should advise parents of the need for their children to wear specific types of clothing on days when your perceptual-motor program is conducted. If you schedule the same days each week for your motor activities, then parental cooperation will be easier to accomplish.

Other safety factors to be taken into consideration are as follows:

1)   Allow only one parson on the equipment at a time.

2)   Insist that students get into a good starting position before beginning any task.

3) Be sure to allow enough space for safe movements.

4) Stress control of movements at all times rather than speed.

5) Insist on strong mental concentration when responding to each challenge. "Showing off" can lead to serious accidents!

PERCEPTUAL-MOTOR EVALUATION SCALE
LEVEL-1

Before beginning any comprehensive program in motor development, participants should be assessed as to their strengths and weaknesses. Obviously there are countless numbers of screening tasks and surveys which are available for use as an assessment instrument. This *Level-1 Perceptual-Motor Evaluation Scale* is provided for teachers because it is easy to administer, takes only a limited amount of instruction time and provides information (as recorded on the *Record Sheet*) which teachers can easily use to plan purposeful program activities. It also provides teachers with a tool which may be used to evaluate student progress and program effectiveness.

GENERAL INSTRUCTIONS

1)   Tests are designed so that they may be administered as a part of the physical education class period.

2)   Do not tell the students they are being "tested". Make the screening a natural part of your physical education period.

3)   Students are given an "S" for Satisfactory Performance and an "N" for Needs Improvement.

4)   Students receiving an "N" should be retested in the middle and/or at the end of your perceptual-motor program.

5)   Demonstration of test items to show correct response is permissible. You are observing performance, not testing ability to interpret verbal directions.

6)   If judgement of a student's performance is uncertain, you may wish to have the student repeat the activity.

7)   Test items may be administered over a period of a few weeks, or over a period of a few days at the teacher's discretion.

8)   Remember....the main purpose of the screening program is to *look* at each student as an individual and as a result, plan program activities which will take into account individual needs.

BODY PARTS

PERFORMANCE OBJECTIVES
By touching specific body parts, student demonstrates body image.

EQUIPMENT

None.

PROCEDURE

Ask student (or students) to stand facing you at a distance of about 10 feet. Student is asked to touch the following body parts: knees, shoulders, hips, head, feet, eyes, elbows, mouth, neck and chest. If students are tested in a group, the eyes must be closed or blindfolded.

EVALUATION

If student makes more than one error in identification, is slow or has to *feel* around to find parts, mark an *N* for *Needs Improvement*.

(knees)

WALKING BOARD

PERFORMANCE OBJECTIVES
By walking forward on a walking board with eyes focused on teacher's hand held at eye level, student demonstrates balance, laterality and visual motor control.

EQUIPMENT

Low walking board and mats.

PROCEDURE

Teacher stands at opposite end of board from student. Ask student to walk the board forward one way with eyes focusing on teacher's hand held at eye level of student.

EVALUATION

If student shows any difficulty such as stepping off board, sliding feet, pausing frequently, or uses a fast walk to avoid losing balance, mark an *N* for *Needs Improvement*.

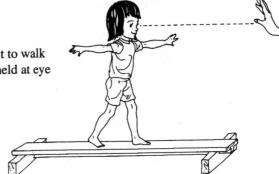

HOPPING

> ### PERFORMANCE OBJECTIVES
> *By pausing and hopping on first the right foot then the left, student demonstrates gross-motor coordination, balance and ability to sustain movement.*

EQUIPMENT

None.

PROCEDURE

Student is asked to support his or her weight on right foot for 3 seconds and then hop forward 3 times in succession on this same foot. Student then turns facing the teacher and supports weight on left foot only for 3 seconds followed by 3 hops in succession on this same foot.

EVALUATION

If opposite foot touches ground while either stationary or hopping, or postural shift is not smooth, lacks rhythm, loses control, etc., mark an *N* for ***Needs Improvement***.

JUMP AND LAND

PERFORMANCE OBJECTIVES
By jumping and landing from a jump box, student demonstrates gross-motor coordination, dynamic balance and kinesthesis.

EQUIPMENT
Jump box with incline board and mats.

PROCEDURE
Student is asked to take jumping position on jump box with feet about shoulder distance apart. (Jump box is 18" to 20" high.) Chair or bench may be used. Student jumps from top of box and lands on mat or other type of soft surface. Student is instructed to jump with both feet leaving jump box at the same time and to land lightly on both feet at the same time without losing balance.

EVALUATION
If both feet do not leave jump box at the same time and land at the same time, or if student is unable to hold balance upon landing, mark an *N* for *Needs Improvement*.

OBSTACLE COURSE

PERFORMANCE OBJECTIVES
*By going over, under and between obstacles,
student demonstrates spatial orientation and body awareness.*

EQUIPMENT
Six chairs and 2 yardsticks or poles.

PROCEDURE
Student is asked to perform 3 tasks:

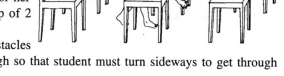

1) Step over an obstacle about as high as his or her knees without touching it (use yardstick across 2 chairs).
2) Duck under an obstacle about 2 inches lower than his or her shoulders without touching it (use yardstick across top of 2 chairs).
3) Squeeze through a narrow opening without touching obstacles (use 2 chairs back to back and place them close enough so that student must turn sideways to get through without touching).

EVALUATION
If the student overestimates or underestimates the space by more than a few inches, or if body contact is made with the obstacle, mark an *N* for *Needs Improvement*.

BALL CATCH

PERFORMANCE OBJECTIVES
*By attempting to catch a ball thrown in an underhand toss by
the teacher, student demonstrates hand-eye coordination and ocular pursuit.*

EQUIPMENT
Ball 7" in diameter.

PROCEDURE
Student is asked to stand facing teacher approximately 6 to 8 feet away. Student forms catching pocket with hands. Teacher tosses a 7" rubber ball to student using an underhand toss. Student attempts to catch the ball using fingers and hands only. Three trials are given to each student.

EVALUATION
If a score of less than 2 catches is made in the 3 trials, mark an N for Needs Improvement. For a fair catch, ball must be caught with fingers and hands and not with arms and body.

OPTIONAL TESTS

The teacher may wish to run an additional screening check on students.
Some examples of optional tests are: Chalkboard, Angels-In-The-Snow and Creeping.

Record all test results
on a copy of the *Record Sheet* example on the next page.
Make as many copies of the *Record Sheet*
as you need for your students.

MARKING N = NEEDS IMPROVEMENT S = SATISFACTORY		Task 1		Task 2		Task 3		Task 4		Task 5		Task 6		Task 7	
		Identify Body Parts		Walking Board		Hopping		Jump and Land		Obstacle Course		Ball Catch		Optional	
No.	NAME	Fall	Spring	Fall	Spring	Fall	Spring	Fall	Spring	Fall	Spring	Fall	Spring	Fall	Spring

WEEKLY LESSONS

Weeks 1 to 25

MAT STUNTS

PERFORMANCE OBJECTIVES
By creeping and crawling, student demonstrates locomotor skill and cross-lateral coordination.

EQUIPMENT

Mats arranged side by side.

CHALLENGES

1) Crawl on your stomach (***alligator crawl***) using bent arms and legs to move your body.
2) Creep forward on your hands and knees.

STRESS: Cross pattern movement forward (right arm moving with left leg, left arm moving with right leg) to coordinate movement efficiently.

ROPE WALKING

PERFORMANCE OBJECTIVES
By walking forward and backward on a rope laid on the floor, student demonstrates balance and tactile awareness.

EQUIPMENT
One or 2 jump ropes.

CHALLENGES
1) Walk forward slowly on top of the rope.
2) Walk backward slowly on top of the rope.
3) Perform a toe-heel **balance walk** forward on top of the rope. (Touch heel of one foot to toes of the other foot while walking the rope.)

STRESS: Walk slowly with head erect and eyes looking straight ahead, ***not*** on feet. Bare feet should be in contact with rope for good kinesthetic and tactile input. (You may wish to tie 2 short ropes together for a longer walk.)

BEAN BAG TOSS INTO TIRES

> ### PERFORMANCE OBJECTIVES
> *By tossing a bean bag into tire targets, student demonstrates hand-eye coordination, laterality, and directionality.*

EQUIPMENT

Classroom set of bean bags and 6 painted bike tires.

CHALLENGES

1) (From behind a restraining line, student is given three underhand tosses on each turn and attempts to get one bean bag into each tire. Student must get bean bag into first tire before trying for 2nd and 3rd tire. Two tossing areas should be used. Use painted bike tires as targets.)

2) (Students successful with preferred hand may be encouraged to try opposite hand.)

STRESS: Stepping forward with opposite foot from throwing hand to transfer weight into toss (cross-lateral pattern) and follow through.

COORDINATION LADDER

PERFORMANCE OBJECTIVES
*By walking between the rungs of a ladder and then on the rungs,
student demonstrates laterality, foot-eye coordination, balance, and space awareness.*

EQUIPMENT
Coordination ladder and mats.

CHALLENGES
1) Walk forward by stepping between the rungs of the ladder.
2) *Balance walk* forward on the rungs of the ladder.
3) Show me a different way of walking over the ladder.

STRESS: Eyes must guide movement! One student goes at a time. Allow repetition
of tasks. *For Safety -* Have the ladder on the rug or mats.

OBSTACLE COURSE

PERFORMANCE OBJECTIVES
By crawling forward on stomach and on back under a series of
obstacles, student demonstrates space awareness, locomotor coordination and body image.

EQUIPMENT

Mats, two cross bars, four cones (or 2 jump standards).

CHALLENGES

1) Crawl forward on your stomach and go under the two cross bar obstacles without touching. (Use mats or rug to crawl on. Use traffic cones with cross tube or jump standards for obstacles.)
2) Crawl forward, but pass under the obstacles on your back without touching.
3) Find a different way of crawling under the obstacles.

STRESS: Use of arms and legs in coordination for efficient movement pattern. Keep body tight against the mat when passing under the obstacle.

JUMPING PATTERNS WITH TIRES

PERFORMANCE OBJECTIVES
*By jumping with both feet, student demonstrates locomotor
coordination, space awareness, foot-eye coordination and kinesthetic awareness.*

EQUIPMENT
Twelve hoops or bike tires.

Pattern 1

Pattern 2

CHALLENGES
1) *PATTERN 1* - Jump forward while placing both feet in each tire.
2) *PATTERN 2* - Jump forward by alternating both feet in the first tire with one foot in each of 2 tires side by side (***straddle jump***) as you jump through the pattern.
3) (After several repetitions of the above directed movements at each pattern, challenge the students to move through the tires in a different way. Hoops may be used in place of tires.)

STRESS: Bend knees, push from toes and use arm thrust for good jumping action. Both feet leave the surface at the same time on the jump.

LOW WALKING BOARD

PERFORMANCE OBJECTIVES
By walking across a low walking board, balancing on one foot and continuing to walk, student demonstrates visual-motor control, balance and laterality.

EQUIPMENT
   Low walking board and mats.

CHALLENGES
   1)   Walk forward to the end of the board with your eyes focusing on the target (teacher's hand).
   2)   Walk forward, balance on one foot at the center of the board (***stork balance***) then continue walking to the end of the board.

STRESS: Walk the board slowly, head erect, eyes on target. Use arms to adjust body weight.

MAT STUNTS

PERFORMANCE OBJECTIVES
*By creeping forward and backward on mat, student demonstrates
gross-motor coordination, cross laterality, tactile and kinesthetic awareness.*

EQUIPMENT
Mats.

CHALLENGES
1) *REVIEW* - Creep forward on your hands and knees.
2) Creep backward on your hands and knees.

STRESS: *REVIEW* - Hands and fingers pointing forward, feet dragging on mat, knees lifting slightly off mat and cross patterning.

BALL BOUNCING WITH TIRES

PERFORMANCE OBJECTIVES
By bouncing and catching a ball in tire openings, student demonstrates hand-eye coordination.

EQUIPMENT
Ball and 5 bike tires in a line.

CHALLENGES
1) Bounce and catch the ball once in each of 5 tires placed side by side while walking outside of the tires.
2) Walk with your feet on top of the tires while bouncing and catching the ball inside of the tires.
3) Find a different way of moving while bouncing and catching the ball inside of each tire.

STRESS: Use of bounce and catch, not a dribble. Form a pocket with the hands and spread the fingers to properly catch the ball. Eyes focus on the target. Push the ball down, not just dropping it.

COORDINATION LADDER

PERFORMANCE OBJECTIVES
*By creeping and then walking between the rungs of a ladder flat on
the floor, student demonstrates space awareness, motor planning ability and laterality.*

EQUIPMENT
   Coordination ladder and mats.

CHALLENGES
   1) Creep on your hands and knees between the rungs of the ladder.
   2) Walk backwards between the rungs of the ladder.
   3) Show me a different way of moving between the rungs of the ladder.

STRESS: Student carefully places limbs into spaces between the rungs of the ladder resting on a mat or carpet. Student move
   only as fast as he or she can maintain control.

OBSTACLE COURSE

PERFORMANCE OBJECTIVES

*By following directions for moving "over", "under", and "through" obstacles,
student demonstrates body and space awareness, directionality and locomotor coordination.*

EQUIPMENT

Mats, car tire with tire holder and 2 cross bars (or jump standards).

CHALLENGES

1) Jump over the cross bar from a *stationary* position.
2) Crawl under the low cross bar (student in prone position).
3) Crawl through the auto tire supported in the tire holder.
4) (After students have been successful on several trials with the above challenges, ask them to find a different way of going through the obstacle course.)

STRESS: Student attempts *not* to touch any obstacles. The height of the cross bars are varied so that the challenge becomes more difficult and requires greater body control.

GEOMETRIC SHAPES

PERFORMANCE OBJECTIVES

By identifying 4 geometric shapes (circle, square, triangle and rectangle) while crawling through them, student demonstrates form perception, space awareness and listening ability.

EQUIPMENT

Classroom set of geometric shapes with holders.

CHALLENGES

1) (Students explore the shapes by crawling through them.) See how many different shapes you can go through.

2) (Present a verbal challenge using one task only.) Can you crawl through a circle (square, rectangle, triangle)? (Challenge only one or two students at a time when using a single task.)

STRESS: Students should be in a creeping position when responding to a challenge. They should attempt to go through the shape without touching it with their bodies.

LOW WALKING BOARD

PERFORMANCE OBJECTIVES
By walking across a walking board that has an obstacle placed over it, student demonstrates visual-motor coordination, laterality and balance.

EQUIPMENT

Low walking board, cross bar and mats.

CHALLENGES

1) *REVIEW: STORK BALANCE* - Walk forward, balance one foot at the center of the board (**stork balance**), then continue walking to the end of the board.

2) *CROSS BAR OBSTACLE* - Walk forward and step over the cross bar placed across the center of the walking board. (Reminder: Cross bar consists of 2 traffic cones with attaching cross tube.)

STRESS: *CROSS BAR OBSTACLE* - Eyes focus on the obstacle (cross bar) which provides visual cues. Walk slowly!

MAT STUNTS

PERFORMANCE OBJECTIVES
By walking "four-legged" and "three-legged", student demonstrates laterality, locomotor coordination, upper arm and shoulder strength, tactile and kinesthetic awareness.

Dog Walk   **Lame Dog Walk**

EQUIPMENT
Mats.

CHALLENGES
1) *DOG WALK - **Dog walk*** on your hands and feet. You perform a ***dog walk*** by doing a 4-legged walk with your weight distributed evenly on your hands and feet.

2) *LAME DOG WALK - **Lame dog walk*** on two hands and one leg. You perform a ***lame dog walk*** by doing a 3-legged walk with your weight on your hands and hopping one of your legs forward while the other leg is held in the air.

STRESS: Weight forward on the hands and arms. Move only as fast as complete body control and coordination can be maintained.

JUMPING PATTERN WITH OBSTACLES

PERFORMANCE OBJECTIVES
By jumping over an obstacle and into designated tires, student demonstrates locomotor coordination, balance, space awareness, and visual-motor control.

EQUIPMENT

Mats, cross bar and four bike tires with one painted red.

Pattern 1

CHALLENGES

1) *PATTERN 1* - Jump over the cross bar and freeze in the red tire (red means stop), then continue jumping through the pattern. (Use two traffic cones with the cross tube and four bike tires.)

2) *PATTERN 2* - Jump through the tires and over the cross bar, catch your weight (*freeze*) in the red tire, then continue through the pattern.

Pattern 2

STRESS: Good jumping form with bent knees on takeoff and landing. Concentrate on the landing with complete balance and control when going over the cross bar.

GEOMETRIC SHAPES

PERFORMANCE OBJECTIVES
By crawling through designated shape and describing one or more things about
it, student demonstrates form perception, space awareness, body image, and serial memory ability.

EQUIPMENT
Classroom set of geometric shapes with holders.

CHALLENGES

1) (Verbal challenge using shape, size and/or color. Example: "Show me how you can crawl through the largest rectangle.")
2) (Verbal challenge using two tasks for those students needing greater challenge. Example: "Can you crawl through a circle and then a triangle?")

STRESS: Careful listening and making body adjustments to size of shape so that no contact is made.

JUMP BOX

PERFORMANCE OBJECTIVES
*By walking and running up an incline board, jumping from a box and landing
on both feet, student demonstrates dynamic balance, locomotor control and self confidence.*

EQUIPMENT

Jump box with incline board and mats.

CHALLENGES

1) Walk up the incline board onto the jump box, take the correct jumping position, release with both feet at once and land on the mat.
2) Carefully run up the incline board and jump from the box onto the mat.

STRESS: Controlled landing (catch weight and *freeze*) with knees bent, land *softly* on the front part of the feet. Use mats for safety and allow as much free space as possible for movement to take place.

CRISSCROSS WALKING PATTERN

PERFORMANCE OBJECTIVES
By walking a rope using a crossover step, student demonstrates laterality, balance, visual-motor control and foot-eye coordination.

EQUIPMENT
One or more jump ropes and two bike tires.

CHALLENGES
1) Start with both feet in the tire and walk the length of the rope 12 to 14 feet long using a crossover step until reaching the opposite tire.
2) Dog walk on your hands and feet (with rope between the hands and the feet) and use a crisscross pattern with only your hands crossing over the rope.

STRESS: Walk slowly, eyes looking ahead and not at the feet, thinking and then moving.

LOW WALKING BOARD

PERFORMANCE OBJECTIVES
By walking across a low walking board carrying a balance pole, student demonstrates dynamic balance and bilaterality.

EQUIPMENT
Low walking board, cross bar, balance pole and mats.

CHALLENGES
1) *REVIEW: CROSS BAR OBSTACLE* - Walk forward and step over the cross bar placed across the center of the board.
2) *BALANCE POLE* - Walk forward carrying a balance pole using an overhand grip with your hands placed slightly wider than shoulder distance apart. (Broom handle may be used as a balance pole.)

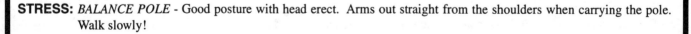

STRESS: *BALANCE POLE* - Good posture with head erect. Arms out straight from the shoulders when carrying the pole. Walk slowly!

MAT STUNTS

PERFORMANCE OBJECTIVES
By walking while clasping ankles with hands, student demonstrates laterality, balance, and kinesthetic awareness.

EQUIPMENT
    Mats.

CHALLENGES
1) *REVIEW: DOG WALK* - Walk 4-legged on your hands and feet.
2) *GORILLA WALK* - Bend over and grasp your ankles with your hands, then move one leg at a time while keeping your legs fairly straight.

STRESS: Proper positioning of body parts. Movement starts and finishes on mats.

HOOP PATTERN WITH BALL BOUNCING

PERFORMANCE OBJECTIVES
By jumping and bouncing and catching a ball inside a hoop a directed number of times, student demonstrates eye-hand coordination, memory sequencing ability and locomotor skill.

EQUIPMENT
  Ball and 4 hoops.

CHALLENGES
  1) (Student holds ball, jumps into each hoop, and bounces and catches the ball a directed number of times inside each hoop.)
  2) (Students successful with a jump may wish to try a hop on one foot while bouncing and catching the ball.)

STRESS: Student should verbalize (count out loud) the number of bounces in each hoop (student jumps from hoop to hoop).

COORDINATION LADDER

PERFORMANCE OBJECTIVES
*By running between the rungs of a coordination ladder and walking with one foot on
each side rail of the ladder, student demonstrates foot-eye coordination, balance, and space awareness.*

EQUIPMENT
Coordination ladder and mats.

CHALLENGES
1) Carefully run between the rungs of the ladder.
2) **Balance walk** with one foot on the top of each side rail of the ladder.
3) Create your own pattern of movement on the ladder.

STRESS: Move only as fast as complete body control can be maintained. "Thought process stays ahead of movement." (As always, ladder is placed on mats or a rug.)

OBSTACLE COURSE

PERFORMANCE OBJECTIVES
By moving under and through obstacles without touching them,
student demonstrates body and space awareness, directionality and locomotor control.

EQUIPMENT
Car tire with holder and 2 cross bars.

CHALLENGES

1) Crawl under the first cross bar.
2) Crawl through the car tire supported in the tire box.
3) Crawl under the 2nd cross bar placed at a lower level than the first bar.
4) (Students successful with the above tasks should be challenged to change their style of body movement.)

under ➡ *through* ➡ *under*

STRESS: Student attempts not to touch any obstacles. Height of the cross bars are varied so that the challenge becomes more difficult and requires greater body control.

JUMP BOX

PERFORMANCE OBJECTIVES
By jumping from a height into a designated target and landing on both feet in an upright position, student demonstrates dynamic balance, space awareness and locomotor skill.

EQUIPMENT
> Jump box with incline board, red bike tire and mats.

CHALLENGES
1) Walk up the incline board onto the jump box, take the correct jumping position, release both feet at once and jump into the *red* tire. (Catch weight with good balance and freeze inside of the tire.)
2) Do it again, but this time carefully run up the incline board.

STRESS: Correct landing with bent knees. *Red* means stop and control the body inside of the tire. (As always, use mats for safety.)

LOW AND INTERMEDIATE WALKING BOARDS

PERFORMANCE OBJECTIVES
By walking across a low walking board and stepping over a series of 4 bean bags, student demonstrates balance, laterality, visual-motor control and tactile awareness.

EQUIPMENT
Low and intermediate walking boards, balance pole, 4 bean bags and mats.

CHALLENGES
This is the first lesson in which two walking boards are used. One at low level (about 7" high) and one at intermediate level (about 13 1/2" high).

1) *REVIEW: INTERMEDIATE BOARD* - Walk forward carrying a balance pole with arms extended from your shoulders.

2) *LOW BOARD* - Walk forward and step over 4 bean bags spaced evenly along the board without looking at your feet.

STRESS: LOW BOARD - Eyes do not watch feet, but may look ahead at the bean bags. Arms help to adjust body weight and position. *REVIEW: INTERMEDIATE BOARD* - Students not ready for the intermediate board stay on the low board.

MAT STUNTS

PERFORMANCE OBJECTIVES
By performing a frog jump, student demonstrates bilaterality, kinesthetic awareness and dynamic balance.

EQUIPMENT
  Mats.

CHALLENGES
  1) *REVIEW: GORILLA WALK* - Grasp your ankles with your hands and walk.
  2) *FROG JUMP* - Squat and place your hands flat on the mat inside of your legs. Push from your toes and spring from the mat with your hands leaving the mat ahead of your feet. Land in a squat position on your feet.

STRESS: *FROG JUMP* - Arms kept straight with hands close together. Takeoff and landing is on the balls of the feet.

HOOP MOVEMENT PATTERN

PERFORMANCE OBJECTIVES
By moving in the same direction around a pattern (lazy eight) using various modes of locomotion, student demonstrates visual memory ability and directionality.

EQUIPMENT

Two hoops.

CHALLENGES

1) Walk around the lazy eight pattern.
2) Creep around the lazy eight pattern.
3) Jump around the lazy eight pattern.

STRESS: Student follows a lazy eight movement pattern (as indicated by the arrows) two times without stopping on each turn for each of the challenges.

COORDINATION LADDER

PERFORMANCE OBJECTIVES
*By moving through the openings of a ladder held on its side without
touching it, student demonstrates space awareness, directionality and body awareness.*

EQUIPMENT

    Coordination ladder and mats.

CHALLENGES

1)   Creep in and out of the windows of the ladder on its side. (Ladder should
      be held in place.)

2)   Show me a different way of going in and out of the windows of the ladder. (Example: moving backwards, or going
      through every other window, etc.)

STRESS: Student attempts to go through openings without touching parts of the ladder. If the students are moving too slowly,
      have them skip every other space.

OBSTACLE COURSE

PERFORMANCE OBJECTIVES
By moving through a more complex obstacle course and making necessary body adjustments, student demonstrates body and space awareness, directionality and locomotor control.

EQUIPMENT

Car tire with holder, two cross bars, two chairs and mats.

CHALLENGES

1) Jump over the cross bar.
2) Crawl under the second cross bar.
3) Walk between the chairs. (Put the chairs close enough to force the student to walk sideways between the chairs.)
4) Go through the tire.
5) Find a new way of moving through the obstacles. (Do this challenge only after a couple of trials of the above challenges.)

STRESS: Student must make the correct body adjustments as he or she relates to the obstacles.

REBOUND NET AND LAUNCHING BOARD

PERFORMANCE OBJECTIVES
By throwing a bean bag at a net and having it rebound at chest height, and by stepping on a board to launch a bean bag so that it returns at waist height, student demonstrates hand-eye coordination and foot-eye coordination.

EQUIPMENT
Rebound net, launching board and classroom set of bean bags.

CHALLENGES
1) *REBOUND NET* - (Student uses an ***overhand*** throw and attempts to hit the center of the net with the bean bag. Student takes a position on the knees so that the bean bag will rebound at chest height. The student is ***not*** instructed to catch the bean bag. Emphasis is on accurate throwing with the bean bag rebounding to the chest. Allow 5 to 10 trials per turn. Use several bags!)

2) *LAUNCHING BOARD* - (Student steps on the end of the board using the heel of the preferred foot and launches the bean bag so that it rebounds at about waist height. Student is ***not*** instructed to catch the bean bag, but may do so if adequate skill is available. Emphasis is on consistently applying enough force to launch the bean bag up to catching height. Allow 5 to 10 trials per turn. Bean bag should be positioned sideways across the board.)

STRESS: *REBOUND NET* - Elbow of the throwing arm held up even with the shoulder. A soft throw should be used with the bean bag striking the chest. *LAUNCHING BOARD* - Student steps on the end of the board using the heel of the foot to provide adequate force.

LOW AND INTERMEDIATE WALKING BOARDS

PERFORMANCE OBJECTIVES
*By maneuvering into and over obstacles on a walking
board, student demonstrates balance, laterality and visual-motor control.*

EQUIPMENT
Low and intermediate walking boards, 4 bean bags, 2 bike tires, cross bar and mats.

CHALLENGES
1) *REVIEW: INTERMEDIATE BOARD* - Walk forward and step over the four bean bags
   spaced evenly along the board.
2) *LOW BOARD* - Walk forward, step into the tires and over the cross bar.

STRESS: Eyes shift from one visual target to another, but do not watch the feet.
Movements on the board are performed slowly.

MAT STUNTS

PERFORMANCE OBJECTIVES
*By rolling across a mat coordinating shoulders, hips and knees,
student demonstrates kinesthetic and tactile awareness, body image and agility.*

EQUIPMENT

Mats.

CHALLENGES

1) *REVIEW: FROG JUMP* - Squat and spring from the mat on all fours.
2) *LOG ROLL* - Lay across the mat on your stomach with your body straight. Your Shoulders, hips, and knees move together in coordination as your body rolls over like a log down the center of the mat.

STRESS: *LOG ROLL* - Hips direct movement of the ***log roll***. Legs and arms are kept straight.

JUMP BOX

PERFORMANCE OBJECTIVES
By moving up an incline board and jumping into a designated tire, student demonstrates dynamic balance, kinesthetic awareness, space awareness and directionality.

EQUIPMENT
Jump box with incline board, 3 bike tires and mats.

CHALLENGES
1) Walk up the incline board onto the jump box, take a good jumping position with your feet spread, release both feet at once and jump into the tire of your choice. (Three tires are used.)
2) This time, carefully ***run*** up the incline board and perform the same tasks.

STRESS: Purposeful movement with full body control.
Student catches weight with soft landing on the balls of the feet in the tire of choice.

GEOMETRIC SHAPES

PERFORMANCE OBJECTIVES
By recognizing four basic geometric shapes, their sizes (small or large), colors (red, green, etc.), and by selecting the appropriate shape upon request, student demonstrates listening skills, form perception, serial memory ability and tactile awareness.

EQUIPMENT

Classroom set of geometric shapes.

CHALLENGES

1) (Use shapes placed flat on the floor without support stands. Provide verbal challenges such as: "Can you walk a large rectangle?" "Show me how you can hop two times inside a small circle." Etc.)

2) (For students needing a greater challenge, use two tasks in sequence. Examples are: "Can you jump three times inside of a square, then walk backwards on a triangle?" "Who can balance on one hand and foot inside a green square?" Etc.)

STRESS: Thinking before moving! Slow movements when walking on the shapes.

JUMPING PATTERN WITH OBSTACLES

PERFORMANCE OBJECTIVES
By jumping over obstacles and into bicycle tire targets, student demonstrates locomotor coordination, directionality, space awareness, dynamic balance and kinesthetic awareness.

EQUIPMENT
Mats, 2 cross bars and 5 bike tires with one tire painted red.

CHALLENGES

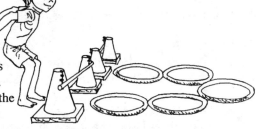

1) Jump over the cross bar and land in the red tire then do long jumps into 4 additional tires with a final jump over the second cross bar.

2) (For variation, if time allows, change spacing of the tires and the height of the cross bars or use other combinations.)

STRESS: Low bending of the knees on takeoff and landing. Soft, light landing with full body control.

BALL BOUNCING AROUND OBSTACLES

PERFORMANCE OBJECTIVES
By bouncing and catching a ball while moving around a series of obstacles, student demonstrates hand-eye coordination, directionality and space awareness.

EQUIPMENT
Ball and 3 traffic cones.

CHALLENGES
1) Using both of your hands, bounce and catch the ball while walking around the traffic cone obstacles.
2) (For students needing a greater challenge, have them dribble the ball using one hand as they walk around the obstacles.)

STRESS: Student must follow the directed pattern, and moves only as fast as good ball control can be maintained. Finger tips control the ball!

LOW AND INTERMEDIATE WALKING BOARDS

PERFORMANCE OBJECTIVES
By walking sideways across a walking board, student demonstrates balance and laterality.

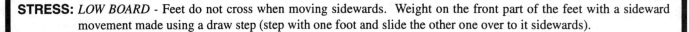

EQUIPMENT
Low and intermediate walking boards, cross bar, 2 bike tires and mats.

CHALLENGES
1) *REVIEW: INTERMEDIATE BOARD* - Walk forward on the intermediate walking board, step into the tires and over the cross bar.
2) *LOW BOARD* - Walk sideward leading with your right foot to the end of the low walking board and back to the starting position leading with your left foot.

STRESS: *LOW BOARD* - Feet do not cross when moving sidewards. Weight on the front part of the feet with a sideward movement made using a draw step (step with one foot and slide the other one over to it sidewards).

MAT STUNTS

PERFORMANCE OBJECTIVES
By changing levels in body position on instruction, student demonstrates body image, kinesthetic and tactile awareness and agility.

EQUIPMENT
   Mats.

CHALLENGES
   1) *REVIEW: LOG ROLL* - Starting position is on your stomach, keep your body straight with your hips leading the movement.
   2) LAY OUT - Everyone kneel across the mat with your arms extended under your shoulders, your hands flat on the mat, and your knees under your hips. On my signal (whistle or clap) everyone ***lay out*** flat on the mat with the palm of your hands slapping the mat. (This is a reaction drill in which students change levels of body positioning.)

STRESS: *LAY OUT* - Hands break the fall. Student should assume good starting position before the stunt begins.

HOPPING PATTERNS WITH ROPES AND HOOPS

PERFORMANCE OBJECTIVES
By hopping over ropes and hoops without losing balance, student demonstrates gross-motor coordination, balance, eye-foot coordination and space awareness.

EQUIPMENT

Four jump ropes and 4 hoops.

CHALLENGES

1) PATTERN 1 - (Ropes are placed in a parallel pattern.) Hop over the ropes and into the spaces between the ropes on your right foot, then on your left foot. Do this without losing your balance.

2) PATTERN 2 - (Hoops are placed side by side in a straight line.) Hop into each hoop first on your right foot then on your left foot without losing your balance.

STRESS: Light movements with the proper use of the arms. Good body alignment (shoulders back with weight supported on one leg only).

GEOMETRIC SHAPES

PERFORMANCE OBJECTIVES
By matching recognition of a geometric shape pictured on a card with a geometric shape on the floor, student demonstrates visual memory ability, form perception and space awareness.

EQUIPMENT
Classroom set of geometric shapes with holders and drawings of basic shapes.

CHALLENGES
1) (Visual challenges using cards with basic shapes drawn on them. Use one, 2, or 3 tasks depending on ability of students. Example: Hold up a card showing a square and then a card showing a circle, etc. Student crawls through the appropriate shape.)

2) (You may wish to add color to the challenge by holding up a blue circle, red rectangle, green square, etc. And by taping colored paper to the shapes corresponding to the color of the shape on the cards.)

STRESS: Student should verbalize (say out loud) the names of the shapes as the cards are held up for response. You may also wish to have the student verbalize the name of the shape as he or she crawls through it.

JUMP BOX

PERFORMANCE OBJECTIVES
By jumping from a height into a specific spatial target, student demonstrates dynamic balance, foot-eye coordination and space awareness.

EQUIPMENT
Jump box with incline board, 6 bike tires and mats.

CHALLENGES
1) Walk up the incline board onto the jump box, take the correct jumping position, release both of your feet at once and land with one foot inside each of the tire targets nearest to the jump box. Then continue jumping through the tire pattern with complete body control.
2) Run up the incline board and perform the same task again.

STRESS: *Soft* and controlled landing. Good starting position on the jump box. Eyes on the tire targets.

REBOUND NET AND LAUNCHING BOARD

PERFORMANCE OBJECTIVES
By throwing and catching a bean bag, and by launching and catching a bean bag, student demonstrates hand-eye and foot-eye coordination.

EQUIPMENT
Rebound net and launching board with classroom set of bean bags.

CHALLENGES
1) *REBOUND NET* - Throw the bean bag overhand to the net so that the bean bag bounces off the net and hits your chest. Trap the bean bag against your chest with your hands. (Best to have the student in a kneeling position about 3-4 feet away. Allow 5-10 trials. More skillful students will be ready to start catching with just the hands Fingers are pointed up, thumbs in close together, forming a pocket in which to catch the bean bag.)

2) *LAUNCHING BOARD* - Step on the end of the board by pushing down on the heel of your preferred foot, launch and catch the bean bag at about waist height. (Allow 5-10 trials. Ask student to see how many in a row he can catch without a miss.)

STRESS: *REBOUND NET* - Student uses "soft" throw and allows bean bag to hit against chest area. *LAUNCHING BOARD* - Student must "watch" bean bag fall into hands. Catching pocket is formed by using hands and fingers with palms facing up.

LOW AND INTERMEDIATE WALKING BOARDS

PERFORMANCE OBJECTIVES
*By moving across a walking board, picking up a bean bag
and supporting bag on head, student demonstrates balance and laterality.*

EQUIPMENT
Low and intermediate walking boards, bean bag and mats.

CHALLENGES

1) *REVIEW: INTERMEDIATE BOARD* - Walk sideways leading with your right foot to the end of the board and back to your starting position leading with your left foot.
2) *LOW BOARD* - Walk forward to the center of the board, pick up the bean bag, place it on your head and walk to the end of the board.

STRESS: *LOW BOARD* - Student should bend knees and lower body down to pick up the bean bag, not stooping from waist with eyes looking forward and not down at feet.

MAT STUNTS

PERFORMANCE OBJECTIVES
By performing a rabbit hop, student demonstrates bilateral coordination and body awareness.

EQUIPMENT
Mats.

CHALLENGES
1) *REVIEW: LAY OUT* - Get on your hands and knees with your hands placed flat on the mat directly under your shoulders. When I signal, flatten your body out into a prone position.
2) *RABBIT HOP* - Squat down with your hands placed flat on the mat and your knees together between your arms. Now reach forward with your hands and jump your feet up to your hands.

STRESS: *RABBIT HOP* - Hands move first followed by feet. Knees and feet are kept together.

JUMPING PATTERN WITH OBSTACLES

PERFORMANCE OBJECTIVES
By jumping and "freezing" in designated target, student demonstrates locomotor control, balance and foot-eye coordination.

EQUIPMENT
Mats, 3 cross bars and 8 bike tires with 3 of them painted red.

CHALLENGES
1) *PATTERN 1* - Jump over the cross bar and *freeze* in the red tire, then continue jumping through the pattern using a *straddle jump* (left foot in left tire and right foot in right tire) and a regular jump into the last tire.
2) PATTERN 2 - Jump into the tire, over the first cross bar, *freeze* in the *red* tire, jump into the next tire, over the second cross bar and *freeze* in the *red* tire.

STRESS: Stopping in the *red* tires with full body control. (As mentioned before, *red* is used as a symbol for stop as in a stop light. The *red* tire indicates that the student must stop and control his or her body within the tire.)

Copyright © Jack Capon 1998

COORDINATION LADDER

PERFORMANCE OBJECTIVES
By jumping between, and by walking with hands and feet on and
between rungs of ladder, student demonstrates locomotor skill, balance and space awareness.

EQUIPMENT

Coordination ladder and mats.

CHALLENGES

1) Jump between the rungs of the ladder.
2) Do a *four-legged walk* on your hands and feet between or on the rungs of the ladder.
3) Show me a different way of moving on the ladder.

STRESS: Both feet leave the ground at the same time on the jump. Student carefully guides feet so that they do not trip on the rungs of the ladder resting on the mats or rug.

OBSTACLE COURSE

PERFORMANCE OBJECTIVES
*By following directions in moving through a series of obstacles,
student demonstrates spacial awareness, directionality, body image and locomotor control.*

EQUIPMENT
Car tire with holder, 2 cross bars, red bike tire and mats.

CHALLENGES
1) Crawl under the cross bar.
2) Go through the car tire.
3) Hop over the cross bar.
4) Land in the *red* tire and catch your weight on one foot.

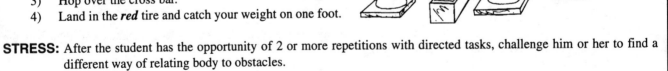

STRESS: After the student has the opportunity of 2 or more repetitions with directed tasks, challenge him or her to find a different way of relating body to obstacles.

BALL ROLLING AT PIN TARGET

PERFORMANCE OBJECTIVES
By rolling a ball at a target (bowling pin) and knocking it over, student demonstrates hand-eye coordination and cross laterality.

EQUIPMENT

Two balls and bowling pins.

CHALLENGES

1) Use two hands to roll the rubber ball at the bowling pin target and knock it over. (Allow two or three tries per turn.)

2) After using two hands to roll the rubber ball, try using one hand. (Have at least two pin targets set up for greater involvement.)

STRESS: Follow-through with rolling hand or hands and stepping forward with opposite foot of rolling hand for proper weight transference. Eyes focus on the target!

LOW AND INTERMEDIATE WALKING BOARDS

PERFORMANCE OBJECTIVES
By walking over a coiled rope obstacle on a walking board, student demonstrates balance, visual-motor control and laterality.

EQUIPMENT

Low and intermediate waling boards, bean bag, jump rope and mats.

CHALLENGES

1) *REVIEW: INTERMEDIATE BOARD* - Walk forward to the center of the board, pick up the bean bag, place it on your head, walk to the end of the board.

2) *LOW BOARD* - Walk forward using the ***snake rope*** as a visual target. (Student attempts to step into the spaces provided by the rope which is coiled around the board.)

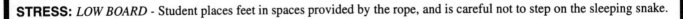

STRESS: *LOW BOARD* - Student places feet in spaces provided by the rope, and is careful not to step on the sleeping snake.

MAT STUNTS

PERFORMANCE OBJECTIVES
*By spinning like a top and remaining upright, student
demonstrates dynamic balance, laterality, directionality and body awareness.*

EQUIPMENT
Mats.

CHALLENGES
1) *REVIEW; RABBIT HOP* - Do a ***rabbit hop*** by squatting with your hands placed flat on the mat and your knees together between your arms.

2) *TOP SPIN* - Do a ***top spin*** by holding your body erect with your feet shoulder distance apart and your hands on your hips. Now spring (jump) from the mat and make a (one fourth, one half, three fourths, or full) turn in mid air and land with full control. (An auditory signal like a whistle, clap, etc., should be used for students to respond. Several students can perform at one time. They are spaced evenly along the length of the mats.)

STRESS: *TOP SPIN* - Student attempts to land with complete balance and control. Feet are kept the same distance apart throughout the stunt. Arms will be needed to help twist the body around on 3/4 and full spins.

REBOUND NET AND LAUNCHING BOARD

PERFORMANCE OBJECTIVES
By catching a bean bag rebounding from the net or launched from the board, student demonstrates hand-eye coordination and foot-eye coordination.

EQUIPMENT
Rebound net, launching board and classroom set of bean bags.

CHALLENGES

1) *REBOUND NET* - (Student is in a standing position. Instructor throws the bean bag against the net and the student catches it using hands and fingers [reaction catching]. Instructor throws fast or slow depending on the student's ability to visually track and catch the bag. Allow 5 to 10 trials for each student. Have enough bags available so that time is not wasted. Student drops bag as soon as caught so that he or she is ready to catch the next one.)

2) *LAUNCHING BOARD* - (Students able to consistently catch the bean bag using 2 hands should be challenged to catch with only one hand. They use their dominant hand. Allow 5 to 10 trials per turn.

STRESS: *REBOUND NET* - Student catches with fingers pointing up. Thumbs are in close. The hands work as a unit and move to the bean bag. *LAUNCHING BOARD* - Eyes visually track (follow) the bean bag into the hand. Hand must move to the bean bag.

GEOMETRIC SHAPES

PERFORMANCE OBJECTIVES
By throwing a bean bag into a designated geometric shape, student demonstrates form perception, hand-eye coordination and kinesthetic awareness.

EQUIPMENT

Classroom set of geometric shapes without supports.

CHALLENGES

1) (Shapes are placed flat on the floor [not supports], and student attempts to toss the bean bags into the shapes.)

2) (Have the student verbally identify the shape into which he or she tosses the bean bag. Allow 4 tosses on each turn. Each time he or she is able to hit a target [shape], he or she then tries for a different shape.)

3) (Another method is for the instructor to challenge the student to toss the bean bag into a specific shape on each trial. Example: "Can you toss the bean bag into the largest square?")

STRESS: Use an underhand throw with a good follow through. Step forward with the opposite foot of the throwing hand.

JUMP BOX

PERFORMANCE OBJECTIVES
By jumping over and landing with control in designated targets, student demonstrates dynamic balance, space awareness, directionality and kinesthetic stimulation.

EQUIPMENT
Jump box with incline board, red bike tire, cross bar and mats.

CHALLENGES
1) Walk up the incline board onto the jump box and take a good jumping position. Now jump forward over a cross bar and land with complete body control.
2) Do it again, only this time jump over the cross bar and land in the *red* bike tire.
3) Do it all again, only this time run up the incline board. (Perform this activity only if additional time is available.)

STRESS: Use of the arms to help lift the body and guide movements. Low bending of the knees to cushion the landing. *Freeze* in the *red* tire with complete body control.

BASIC MOVEMENT SKILLS WITH OBSTACLES

PERFORMANCE OBJECTIVES
*By galloping and skipping around a series of obstacles,
student demonstrates locomotor skill, directionality and space awareness.*

EQUIPMENT

Three traffic cones.

CHALLENGES

1) Show me how you can *gallop* around the cone obstacles.
2) Show me how you can *skip* around the cones.

STRESS: Participants should receive several repetitions of each movement skill. *GALLOP* - One foot leads. Student pushes with the other foot like riding a scooter. *SKIP* - Emphasize a rhythmic step and a hop on alternate feet.

PERFORMANCE OBJECTIVES
*By responding to directions for movement of body limbs while lying in a supine position,
student demonstrates bilateral, unilateral and cross-lateral movement and control and body awareness.*

Use this week for makeup lessons and/or checking the progress of your students on the ***Level-1 Perceptual-Motor Evaluation Scale***. Also, we recommend introducing ***Angels In The Snow*** to your students. It is an excellent activity for developing laterality and body awareness.

Coordinated movements of body limbs, as stressed in ***Angels In The Snow***, help students learn laterality and develop awareness of their bodies. They become aware of their extremities and their positions in space relative to their bodies. Having them make movements in sequence helps them gain good bilateral control in which each side maintains its independence but is integrated with the other.

EQUIPMENT
    None.

DIRECTIONS
1)   Lie on your back on the floor (or mats) with your arms at your sides and your feet together. (Make sure they have room to move their limbs without interference.)
2)   Pretend you are lying in the snow. With your body you will make ***Angels In The Snow***.

3) (You can help students acquire a visual picture of what they are supposed to do by demonstrating with your back to the wall.) See how my arms and legs move against the wall just like yours when they move against the floor.

4) Move your arms up over your head until your hands touch and then move them back to your sides. (Stress that they feel the floor at all times.) Now move your feet apart and back together. Now move your arms and feet apart at the same time. (This drill is just to give them the feeling of dragging their arms and legs against the surface of the floor and to become acquainted with the activity.)

5) (Using directional visual cues such as the windows, the picture wall, the blackboard, the clock wall, etc., direct the students through the sequence that follows. As soon as your students have a good concept of *left* and *right*, use these cues instead of visual cues.)

   a) Move just your right arm. Now move it back to your side.
   b) Move just your left arm. Now move it back to your side.
   c) Move just your right leg. Now back together.
   d) Move just your left leg. Now back together.
   e) Move both arms above your head. Now back to your side (arms on the floor and hands touch).
   f) Move both legs apart. Now move them back together. (Heels remain on the floor.)
   g) Now move your right arms and your right leg at once. Then back.
   h) Now move your left arm and your left leg at once. Then back.
   i) Now move your right arm and your left leg. Then back.
   j) Now move your left arm and your right leg. Then back.

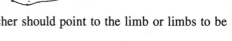

(Please note that if you are working with individual students, the teacher should point to the limb or limbs to be moved by the student.)

EVALUATION

Difficulty with this task indicates that the student is experiencing problems in controlling the parts of his or her body individually or in given combinations. Inadequate performance is shown by:

1) Marked hesitancy in beginning the movements.
2) Restriction of the extent of movement in any of the patterns.
3) Overflow of movements to the limbs not required in the pattern.
4) Inability to interpret tactual cues by pressing against the floor or kinesthetic cues by abortive movements.
5) Inability to carry out any of the patterns.

ACCEPTABLE PERFORMANCE

Student can respond to directions for bilateral, unilateral and cross lateral movements of body limbs while lying in a supine position.

FOR STUDENT HAVING DIFFICULTY

1) Touch the arm or leg to be moved.
2) Actually guide the arm or leg not responding. (Move it through the required range of movement.)
3) Use sensory cues such as weighted or colored objects placed in the hands or on the feet.

LOW AND INTERMEDIATE WALKING BOARDS

PERFORMANCE OBJECTIVES
By moving through an obstacle course on a walking board without touching
the obstacles, student demonstrates dynamic balance, spatial orientation, and directionality.

EQUIPMENT
Low and intermediate walking boards, jump rope, cross bar, hoop and mats.

CHALLENGES
1) *REVIEW: INTERMEDIATE BOARD* - Walk forward using the ***snake rope*** as a visual target. (Student attempts to step into the spaces provided by the rope which is coiled around the board.)
2) *LOW BOARD* - Walk forward, step over the cross bar, make a full turn at the center of the board, go through the hoop and walk to the end of the board.

STRESS: *LOW BOARD* - Make the turn slowly at the center of the board and move through the hoop without touching it. (Hoop must be held up by a participant or an aide.)

MAT STUNTS

PERFORMANCE OBJECTIVES
By moving parts of the body one side at a time as in a bear walk, student demonstrates unilateral coordination, body awareness and balance.

EQUIPMENT
Mats.

CHALLENGES
1) *REVIEW: TOP SPINS* - Jump from the mat, make a one fourth (one half, three fourths, or full) turn in midair and land with full control.
2) *BEAR WALK* - Get down on the mat and put your weight on all four hands and feet. Do not let your knees touch the mat. Move one side of your body forward, then the other.

STRESS: *BEAR WALK* - Hand and foot on one side of the body works as a unit, lifting from the mat and moving forward at the same time.

JUMP BOX

PERFORMANCE OBJECTIVES
By jumping sideways from a height and landing with good control,
student demonstrates laterality, dynamic balance and locomotor coordination.

EQUIPMENT
   Jump box with incline board, red bike tire and mats.

CHALLENGES
1) Walk up the incline board and take a position facing sideways on the jump box. Jump sidewards from the jump box with your right side leading and land with good control and balance.
2) Do it all again but this time jump sidewards with your left side leading.
3) Jump sidewards from the jump box and land in the ***red*** tire. (Instructor should verbally challenge student to lead with the right side or the left side.)

STRESS: Both feet leave the box at the same time on the sideward jump. Knees bend on the takeoff and landing.

GEOMETRIC SHAPES

PERFORMANCE OBJECTIVES
By feeling geometric shapes while blindfolded and identifying them, student demonstrates tactile awareness and form discrimination.

EQUIPMENT
Classroom set of geometric shapes and blindfold.

CHALLENGES
1) (Student is blindfolded—use masks with eyes taped over, if available, and creeps on his or her hands and knees to the shapes under the guidance of a teacher or aide.)
2) Carefully feel the shape with your hands, tell me the name of the shape and then go through it.

STRESS: Student is challenged to use tactile sensory processing and therefore eyes are covered or closed while attempting to identify the shapes.

COORDINATION LADDER

PERFORMANCE OBJECTIVES
By moving across a coordination ladder with different movements,
student demonstrates balance, laterality, space awareness and motor planning ability.

EQUIPMENT
Coordination ladder and mats.

CHALLENGES
1) *BALANCE WALK* - Do a ***balance walk*** on the side rail of the ladder. (Student walks down one side rail of the ladder and returns back to the starting position on the other side rail of the ladder.)
2) *RABBIT HOP* - Do a ***rabbit hop*** between and over the rungs of the ladder.

STRESS: *RABBIT HOP* - Student may place the hands wherever he or she feels most successful, but the feet land in spaces between the rungs of the ladder.

REBOUND NET AND LAUNCHING BOARD

PERFORMANCE OBJECTIVES
By eye-tracking a bean bag and catching it, student demonstrates hand-eye coordination and laterality.

EQUIPMENT
Rebound net and launching board with classroom set of bean bags.

CHALLENGES
1) *REBOUND NET* - Throw the bean bag against the net and try to catch it using your two hands with your fingers pointing up and your hands forming a ***pocket***. Allow 10 trials per turn and challenge the student to see how many catches can be made in succession without a miss.)

2) *LAUNCHING BOARD* - Launch the bean bag from the launching board and catch it with your two hands. (Students able to catch the bean bag consistently using 2 hands should be challenged to use alternate hands. First the left hand and then the right hand, etc. Instructor may wish to challenge more skillful students to use their ***left*** or ***right*** hand as called out.)

STRESS: *REBOUND NET* - Student uses a ***soft*** throw. Change the rebound angle so that the bean bag comes back more slowly. Bean bag is caught out in front of the body, ***not*** against the chest. Opposite foot from the throwing hand should be forward on the throwing motion. *LAUNCHING BOARD* - Hand must move quickly to the bean bag with eyes watching the bean bag from board to hand. Bend knees, if necessary, to lower the body.

LOW AND INTERMEDIATE WALKING BOARDS

PERFORMANCE OBJECTIVES
By walking forward and backward on a walking board,
student demonstrates dynamic balance, laterality and tactile awareness.

EQUIPMENT
Low and intermediate walking boards, cross bar, hoop and mats.

CHALLENGES
1) *REVIEW: INTERMEDIATE BOARD* - Walk forward, step over the cross bar, make a full turn at the center of the board, go through the hoop and walk to the end of the board.
2) *LOW BOARD* - Walk forward to the center of the board, make a half-turn and walk backward to the end of the board.

STRESS: *LOW BOARD* - Student *feels* the board with the toes and then allows the heel to come down when walking backward. Eyes focus on the visual target (teacher's hand, hoop, etc.) *not* on the feet.

MAT STUNTS

PERFORMANCE OBJECTIVES
By performing an egg roll, student demonstrates body image, kinesthetic awareness and locomotor coordination.

EQUIPMENT
Mats.

CHALLENGES

1) *REVIEW: BEAR WALK* - Get down on your hands and feet. Move your body forward by first moving your hands and feet forward on one side of your body and then the other side and then the other side and so on. Don't let your knees touch the ground.

2) *EGG ROLL* - Get in a kneeling position with your arms crossed and your elbows resting on the mat. Now roll over *sideways* across your shoulders and back up to your starting position (kneeling position). Keep your arms crossed at all times. (Student performs a series of three rolls, but must be in a good starting position on each roll.)

STRESS: *EGG ROLL* - The knees are pulled in tight toward the chest as the student rolls across his or her back. Arms stay crossed throughout the roll. Student attempts to maintain starting position with the legs *tucked in* throughout each roll.

BALL DRIBBLING WITH OBSTACLES

PERFORMANCE OBJECTIVES
By dribbling a ball around in a directed pattern and showing ability to control the ball, student demonstrates hand-eye coordination, visual memory and directionality.

EQUIPMENT

Ball and three traffic cones.

CHALLENGES

Dribble the ball with one hand around the cone obstacles in the pattern shown. If you are unable to control the ball with a one-handed dribble, you can try dribbling with both hands. (Students not ready for this task may use a modified bounce and catch. If space is limited, use two cones instead of 3.)

STRESS: Student attempts to follow the directed pattern. Finger tips control the ball using a push and not a slap.

REBOUNDER

PERFORMANCE OBJECTIVES
By marching and jogging on a rebounder, student demonstrates locomotor control and laterality.

EQUIPMENT

Rebounder and mats.

CHALLENGES

1) *CROSS-LATERAL MARCHING* - Stand over the center of the rebounder. March (walk) in place over the center area by using cross-lateral limb movements. In other words, as you march in place, raise your left arm with your right leg then raise your right arm with your left leg. When I give the command to *freeze*, stop in place.

2) *CROSS-LATERAL JOGGING* - Do the same as you did for *marching* except *jog* (light running) over the center area. When I give the command to *freeze*, stop in place.

STRESS: Feet are placed approximately shoulder distance apart to begin the challenges. Eyes focus on the instructor, not down at the feet. Arms move in opposition to leg movement. Place the rebounder on mats (if available) for safety.

OBSTACLE COURSE

PERFORMANCE OBJECTIVES
*By moving through an obstacle course, student
demonstrates body awareness, directionality and locomotor coordination.*

EQUIPMENT
Jump box with incline board, two cross bars, bike tire, car tire with holder and mats.

CHALLENGES
1) Jump from the jump box over the cross bar and land inside the bike tire.
2) Crawl under the low cross bar.
3) Crawl through the car tire.
4) (After a few trials, challenge the students to move through the obstacle course in a different manner.

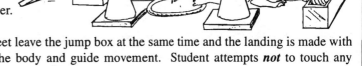

STRESS: Controlled and purposeful movement. Both feet leave the jump box at the same time and the landing is made with both feet at the same time. Arms help lift the body and guide movement. Student attempts *not* to touch any obstacles.

REBOUND NET AND LAUNCHING BOARD

PERFORMANCE OBJECTIVES
*By tossing and launching a ball and catching it on the rebound,
student demonstrates hand-eye and foot-eye coordination and laterality.*

EQUIPMENT
Rebound net, launching board and two tennis balls or two soft rubber balls.

CHALLENGES
1) *REBOUND NET* - Throw the small ball against the net and catch it with your two hands forming a ***pocket***. (Net angle is adjusted to give a softer return. Allow ten trials on each turn.)

2) *LAUNCHING BOARD* - Launch the small ball on the launching board and catch it with two hands. (Students needing a greater challenge should try to clap their hands before catching the ball. Allow 10 trials on each turn.

STRESS: *REBOUND NET* - Ball held near the ear with elbow up at shoulder level. Student steps towards the net with the opposite foot from the throwing hand. Catch is made with fingers up, palms facing forward, thumbs in close and hands forming a pocket. *LAUNCHING BOARD* - Step on the board using the heel of the preferred foot. Hands move as a unit to the ball.

LOW AND INTERMEDIATE WALKING BOARDS

PERFORMANCE OBJECTIVES
*By walking backwards on a walking board without losing balance,
student demonstrates dynamic balance, tactile and kinesthetic awareness and laterality.*

EQUIPMENT

    Low and intermediate walking boards and mats.

CHALLENGES

1) *REVIEW: INTERMEDIATE BOARD* - Walk forward to the center of the intermediate walking board, make a half-turn, and walk backward to the end of the board.

2) *LOW BOARD* - Walk backwards to the end of the low walking board.

STRESS: *LOW BOARD* - Student does not slide feet or turn head. Ask the
student to stop when student *feels* he or she has arrived at the end of
the board.

MAT STUNTS

PERFORMANCE OBJECTIVES
By performing a flip-flop, student demonstrates cross laterality and body awareness.

EQUIPMENT
Mats.

CHALLENGES

1) *REVIEW: EGG ROLL* - Get in a kneeling position with your arms crossed and your elbows resting on the mat. Now roll over sideways to the right across your shoulders and back up to your starting position (kneeling position). Do it again but this time roll to your left. (Have student roll to the right on a series of rolls and then a series to the left.)

2) *FLIP-FLOP* - Get in a prone position, that is, lie down on your stomach with your left hand stretched out beyond your head, your right knee brought forward, and your head turned facing your right hand. (Sometimes referred to as the ***thumb sucking position***.) On my command, ***flip***, your hands and knees should alternate their positions, that is, stretch your right hand beyond your head, move your left knee forward, and turn your head to face your left hand. When I say ***flop***, go back to your starting position. (Allow five to ten repetitions of the full sequence.)

STRESS: *FLIP-FLOP* - Head, arms and legs all change position at the same time. Arms and legs maintain contact with the mat.

JUMPING AND HOPPING PATTERN WITH ROPES & TIRES

PERFORMANCE OBJECTIVES

By jumping with both feet and changing from right foot to left foot while hopping, student demonstrates locomotor control, balance, laterality, directionality and eye-foot coordination.

EQUIPMENT

Ten hoops or bike tires and 4 jump ropes.

CHALLENGES

1) *PATTERN 1* - Jump over the stream (rope) and into the hoop (tire). Continue jumping through the pattern. (Over, into, over, into, etc. Teacher may wish to vary the distance between the obstacles. See rope and hoop pattern.)

2) *PATTERN 2* - Hop into the first two hoops (bike tires) on your right foot, then change to your left foot and continue hopping through the three hoops, then change to your right foot again and continue hopping through the last two hoops. (See hoop pattern.)

STRESS: *PATTERN 1* - Use of the arms in helping to lift and thrust the body forward. *PATTERN 2* - Starting on the correct foot (right foot) and correctly alternating the feet from the right side, to the left side, and to the right side again.

COORDINATION LADDER

PERFORMANCE OBJECTIVES
By walking and bouncing a ball between rungs of a coordination ladder lying
flat on the floor, student demonstrates hand-eye coordination, tactile awareness and balance.

EQUIPMENT
Coordination ladder and ball.

CHALLENGES
1) Walk alongside of the left (or right) side rail of the coordination ladder while bouncing and catching the rubber ball in the spaces between the rungs.
2) Walk with one foot on each side rail of the ladder while bouncing and catching the ball between the rungs. (See illustration.)

STRESS: Eye focusing from the ball to the spatial target and back to the ball, hands maintain a *pocket* and catch with *soft* fingers.

REBOUNDER

PERFORMANCE OBJECTIVES
By rebounding (jumping) on a rebounder and freezing on command,
student demonstrates dynamic balance, body awareness, and locomotor control.

EQUIPMENT
Rebounder and mats.

CHALLENGES

1) *REVIEW: CROSS-LATERAL JOGGING* - Jog or run lightly in place over the center of the rebounder and stop when I say *freeze*. Remember to raise your right arm with your left leg and your left arm with your right leg as you jog.

2) *CONTROLLED REBOUNDING* - Stand over the center of the rebounder and jump five to ten times to get the *feel* of the rebounder. This is called *rebounding*. (Student jumps only over the center of rebounder while keeping body straight and does not lean forward.) On my command to *freeze*, stop in place by letting your knees bend slightly.

STRESS: Feet are placed approximately shoulder distance apart to begin the challenge. All rebounding takes place over the center of the rebounder. Use the arms to help lift the body and maintain balance. Student keeps the head up and does not look down at the feet. *FOR SAFETY* - Do not allow the students to jump from the rebounder onto the floor. They **step down** when dismounting.

STEPPING STONE PATTERN

PERFORMANCE OBJECTIVES
By walking on bean bags (stones) without losing balance,
student demonstrates laterality, directionality, balance and motor planning ability.

EQUIPMENT

Classroom set of bean bags and two hoops or bike tires.

CHALLENGES

(To begin with, use the pattern illustrated, but later make modifications as desired.)

1) Walk from one hoop to the other by stepping on the stones (bean bags) in the stream on the floor. Be careful not to lose your balance and step in the stream (floor and/or rope). (Rope represents the center of a stream of water; student is challenged not to get the feet wet. Student must walk as shown in the pattern.)

2) Walk backwards on the stones in the stream.

STRESS: Student attempts to maintain good balance and motor plans (thinks) ahead.

LOW AND INTERMEDIATE WALKING BOARDS

PERFORMANCE OBJECTIVES
*By walking forward on a slanted walking board,
student demonstrates balance and tactile and kinesthetic awareness.*

EQUIPMENT

Low and intermediate walking boards and mats.

CHALLENGES

1) *REVIEW: INTERMEDIATE BOARD* - Walk backward to the end of the board maintaining good posture.

2) *LOW BOARD* - (Remove one support and make it into an incline board.) Walk forward to the end of the board (upward), make a half turn and return to your starting position.

STRESS: *LOW BOARD* - Student does not look at feet. Student should focus on the instructor's hand.

MAT STUNTS

PERFORMANCE OBJECTIVES
By executing a forward roll, student demonstrates gross-motor coordination, body awareness and balance.

EQUIPMENT
Mats

CHALLENGES
1) *REVIEW: FLIP-FLOP* - Get down on your stomachs in a prone position and do a *flip-flop* at my command. Remember to quickly reverse the positions of your arms and legs when I say *flip* and *flop*.

2) *FORWARD ROLL* - Start in a squat position by sitting on your heels with your hands flat on the mat and your knees together inside of your arms. (Students can be reminded that this is also the starting position for the *rabbit hop*.) Now tuck your chin against your knees, then raise your hips up high, push with your toes, lower the back of your head to the mat and roll over while keeping tucked in a round position like a ball. (Have students practice basic positioning by using the verbal cues: *tuck chin*, *lift hips*. They must acquire a feeling of the hips leading the body over with the head staying tucked.)

STRESS: *FORWARD ROLL* - Hands are flat on the mat for solid support and do not move forward as the roll is started.

Toes are placed up to the edge of the mat for the starting position.

JUMP BOX

PERFORMANCE OBJECTIVES
By jumping and turning body part way in a given direction, student demonstrates dynamic balance, directionality, locomotor coordination and space awareness.

EQUIPMENT
Jump box with incline board, 4 bike tires and mats.

CHALLENGES
1) Walk up the incline board and take the correct jumping position with your toes up to the edge of the box. Jump from the box and perform a 1/4 turn to the *left* and land on the mat. Try the same task with a 1/4 turn to the *right*.
2) Perform a 1/4 turn the *left* with one foot landing in each of two tires placed side by side on the left. Try the same task with a 1/4 turn to the *right* with one foot landing in each of two tires placed side by side on the right.
3) Now I will challenge you to perform a 1/4 turn to the left or right and you must land facing in the correct direction and in the correct tires.

STRESS: Student does *not* twist (turn) his or her body until after the forward jump is made. *FOR SAFETY - Do not* place the tires close to the box. Make the student jump out to the tires.

GEOMETRIC SHAPES

PERFORMANCE OBJECTIVES
By identifying basic geometric shapes, and by
responding to a series of commands and performing accordingly,
student demonstrates form perception, hand-eye coordination and serial memory ability.

EQUIPMENT
Classroom set of geometric shapes and ball.

CHALLENGES
(Shapes are placed flat on the floor (no supports) and the student is challenged to bounce and catch the rubber ball inside of designated shapes. For challenges involving color, simply tape a piece of colored paper to a shape. See the following examples:)
1) Can you bounce and catch the ball two times inside of a circle and 3 times inside of a rectangle?
2) Show me how you can bounce and catch the ball one time inside the smallest square and four times inside the blue triangle.
3) Etc.

STRESS: Student should verbalize (identify each shape and count the number of bounces and/or catches out loud) as the ball is bounced into each shape.

REBOUNDER

PERFORMANCE OBJECTIVES
By listening, and then rebounding on a rebounder the number of times
that the ball has been bounced, student demonstrates auditory perception and locomotor control.

EQUIPMENT
   Rebounder, rubber ball, and mats.

CHALLENGES
1) *REVIEW: CONTROLLED REBOUNDING* - Rebound five to ten times on the rebounder.
2) *AUDITORY REBOUNDING* - Listen to the number of times that I bounce the ball on the floor behind your back. When I am through, rebound or jump the same number that the ball was bounced.

STRESS: Student positions body over the center of the rebounder with feet approximately shoulder distance apart to begin the challenge. Discourage high rebounding. Good control is the most import ant factor! *FOR EXTRA SAFETY -* Waiting students should serve as ***spotters*** around the rebounder in case the performer loses control!

REBOUND NET AND LAUNCHING BOARD

PERFORMANCE OBJECTIVES
By catching a thrown or launched bean bag with varieties of dexterity, student demonstrates laterality and hand-eye coordination

EQUIPMENT
Rebound net, launching board and classroom set of bean bags.

CHALLENGES
1) *REBOUND NET* - Show me how you can consistently throw and catch a bean bag using your two hands. Catch the bean bag using only one preferred hand Catch the bean bag with the hand opposite your preferred hand.. (Allow ten trials per turn. Insist on concentrated and purposeful performance.)

2) *LAUNCHING BOARD* - Launch the bean bag from the launching board and clap your hands just before you catch it with one or both hands. Launch the bean bag and snap your fingers just before you catch it with one or both hands. Launch the bean bag and slap your knees just before you catch it with one or both hands. (Allow ten trials per turn.)

STRESS: *REBOUND NET* - Student should take on an aggressive catching style. Hand or hands go out to meet the bean bag. Fingers must be relaxed, not stiff or tense. *LAUNCHING BOARD* - Bean bag launched at least waist high so time is available to perform the task. Heel contacts the board. Hands move under the bean bag to form a catching pocket with the palms up.

LOW AND INTERMEDIATE WALKING BOARDS

PERFORMANCE OBJECTIVES
By walking forward, sideways and backward on a slanted walking board, student demonstrates dynamic balance, laterality, tactile and kinesthetic awareness.

EQUIPMENT
Low and intermediate walking boards and mats.

CHALLENGES
1) *REVIEW: INTERMEDIATE BOARD* - (Remove one support and make it into an incline board.) In an upward direction, walk forward to the end of the board, make a half turn and return to your starting position.
2) *LOW BOARD* - (Remove one support and make it into an incline board.) In an upward direction, walk forward one third of the way, walk sideward one third of the way and then walk backward to the end of the board. Return downward to your starting position using the same pattern of forward, sideward, and backward.

STRESS: *LOW BOARD* - Good body alignment, slow movements and use of both right and left sides leading on the sideward movement.

MAT STUNTS

PERFORMANCE OBJECTIVES

By performing a series of forward rolls and coming to an upright position on each roll, student demonstrates body awareness, gross-motor coordination and dynamic balance.

EQUIPMENT

Mats.

CHALLENGES

1) *REVIEW: FORWARD ROLL* - Get in a squat position, sitting on your heels with your knees between your arms and your hands flat on the mat. Complete the ***forward roll*** to the verbal cues I call out: ***tuck your chin***, ***lift your hips***, and ***roll***.

2) *FORWARD ROLL TO STANDING POSITION* - Stand at attention at the beginning of the mat. Squat on the mat, perform a ***forward roll*** and come right back up to a standing position again. (Have the students perform this activity two more times to complete the series of three.)

STRESS: *FORWARD ROLL TO STANDING POSITION* - A good starting position before each roll is made and keeping ***tucked*** during the roll. Student comes up to the position of ***attention*** before beginning each ***forward roll***.

LONG JUMPING PATTERN WITH OBSTACLES

PERFORMANCE OBJECTIVES
By jumping a specified distance and landing in a
specific target with full body control, student demonstrates directionality,
gross-motor coordination, space awareness, dynamic balance and kinesthetic awareness.

EQUIPMENT
Mats, three cross bars and four bike tires with one of them red.

CHALLENGES

1) Jump over the cross bar and land in the **red** tire. Then jump into the nearest tire and turn your body in the air so you are facing the second cross bar. Jump over the second cross bar and land in a tire. Then jump into the nearest tire and turn your body so you are facing the third cross bar. Jump over the third cross bar. (Distance between the cross bars and tires depends on the ability level of the participants.)

2) (For variation, change the distance between the obstacles and also the height of the cross bars.)

STRESS: Bending of the knees on the take off and landing. Use of arm thrust to help lift and propel the body. *Soft* landing with full body control. Note that it is important that the student adjusts the body position while airborne so that the body is facing the next obstacle upon landing.

SCOOTER BOARD

PERFORMANCE OBJECTIVES
*By moving on a scooter board around an obstacle without knocking it
over, student demonstrates bilateral coordination, balance and kinesthetic awareness.*

EQUIPMENT
Scooter board and bowling pin.

CHALLENGES
1) Take a prone position (lay on your stomach) on the scooter board and use your hands and arms to propel the scooter board around the bowling pin and back to the starting position. Don't knock over the pin!
2) Do the same thing, but this time get on your knees on the scooter board.

STRESS: Body is balanced on the scooter board (feet do not touch the floor), hands and arms work in rhythmic coordination.

REBOUNDER

PERFORMANCE OBJECTIVES
*By listening and then touching body part(s) called out while
continuing to rebound, student demonstrates body awareness and locomotor control.*

EQUIPMENT

Rebounder and mats.

CHALLENGES

1) *REVIEW: AUDITORY REBOUNDING* - Listen to the number of times I bounce the ball on the floor behind your back. Rebound (jump) the same number of times that I bounced the ball.

2) *BODY AWARENESS REBOUNDING* - Begin rebounding on the rebounder. While you're rebounding touch the parts of your body that I call out. (Examples: head, shoulders, knees, etc.) Continue to rebound with good control until I give the command to *freeze*. When you hear me call out *freeze*, stop rebounding and let your knees bend slightly.

STRESS: Movement takes place over the center point of the rebounder. Emphasize controlled rebounding at a low level.
BODY AWARENESS - Student must be careful not to lean too far forward when touching specific body parts. Control can easily be lost!

COORDINATION LADDER

PERFORMANCE OBJECTIVES
By walking on the rungs of a coordination ladder and bouncing a ball between the rungs, student demonstrates hand-eye coordination and balance.

EQUIPMENT
Coordination ladder and a ball.

CHALLENGES
1) Walk on the rungs of the ladder, bounce and catch the ball in the spaces between the rungs.
2) Hold the ball between your knees and jump over and between the rungs of the ladder while trying to keep the ball in control. This is called a ***kangaroo jump***.

STRESS: Slow and deliberate movements while walking on the rungs of the ladder. When doing the ***kangaroo jump***, the ball is held securely between the knees. Arms help to lift the body.

LOW AND INTERMEDIATE WALKING BOARDS

PERFORMANCE OBJECTIVES
*By balancing an object on each hand while walking on a
walking board, student demonstrates laterality and dynamic balance.*

EQUIPMENT

Low and intermediate walking boards, mats and two bean bags.

CHALLENGES

1) *REVIEW: INTERMEDIATE BOARD* - Walk forward on the intermediate board one third of the way, sideward one third of the way, and backward one third of the way to the end of the board. Now turn around and use the same pattern to walk back the way you came. (You can use an incline board or a regular straight walking surface.)

2) *LOW BOARD* - Walk forward to the end of the low board balancing a bean bag on the top of each hand.

STRESS: *LOW BOARD* - Bean bags are carried on the ***back*** of the hands. Head is erect with the shoulders back for good body alignment.

MAT STUNTS

PERFORMANCE OBJECTIVES
By "walking" on hands and feet in an inverted body position (crab walk), student demonstrates body awareness, laterality and upper body strength.

EQUIPMENT
Mats and a bean bag.

CHALLENGES

1) *REVIEW: FORWARD ROLL TO STANDING POSITION* - Stand at the end of the mat. Do three ***forward rolls*** in succession (one after another) down the length of the mat. Come to a standing position after each ***forward roll***.

2) *CRAB WALK* - Start with your body in an inverted position. That is, lie on your back and push your hips and back up into the air with your feet and hands. Make sure your weight is distributed evenly on your feet and hands. In other words, don't push any harder on your feet than you do on your hands and don't let your hips get higher than your shoulders. Start moving in the direction of your head or feet. For those of you who can, put a bean bag on your stomach and move down the mats in the ***crab walk*** position without letting the bean bag fall off.

STRESS: *CRAB WALK* - Trunk of the body should be held up straight and flat like a board.

HOPPING PATTERN WITH ROPES AND TIRES

PERFORMANCE OBJECTIVES
By hopping through obstacle courses without losing balance, student demonstrates locomotor coordination, dynamic balance, space awareness and directionality.

EQUIPMENT
Five jump ropes, cross bar with three bike tires with one tire red.

CHALLENGES

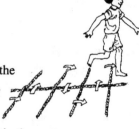

1) *PATTERN 1* - On your right foot only, hop forward over the rope, hop sideward over the rope, hop forward over the rope, hop sideward over the rope, hop forward over the rope, hop sideward over the rope and hop forward over the rope. Go back and do it again but this time hop only on your *left* foot. (Arrows indicate movement pattern.)

2) *PATTERN 2* - On your right foot only, hop over the cross bar and land on your right foot in the *red* tire. *Freeze!* Still hopping on your right foot, hop out of the *red* tire into the second tire, hop out of the second tire into the third and last tire. Go back and do it again but this time hop only on your *left* foot.

STRESS: Arms help to guide movement. Student attempts to keep weight on one foot. *PATTERN 2 - Freeze* in the *red* tire before continuing the movement.

JUMP BOX

PERFORMANCE OBJECTIVES
By jumping from a height, twisting body in midair and landing upright, student demonstrates dynamic balance, body and space awareness and locomotor coordination.

EQUIPMENT
Jump box with incline board, mats and two bike tires.

CHALLENGES
1) Walk up the incline board onto the jump box, take a good jumping position, jump and perform a half turn while you're in the air and land facing ***towards the jump box*** with good balance and control.

2) If you can perform the first activity with good control, you can do it again but this time you may carefully ***run*** up the incline board.

3) (Place two tires on the mat side by side in front of the jump box.) Walk up the incline board, jump off the jump box, in midair make a half turn and land with one foot inside of each tire.

STRESS: Student jumps out away from the jump box and does not twist (turn) body until after forward jump is made. Make sure the mats are used to land on for safety.

BALL DRIBBLING IN HOOPS

PERFORMANCE OBJECTIVES
By jumping from hoop to hoop and dribbling a ball a specified number of times in each hoop, student demonstrates locomotor skills, hand-eye coordination and memory sequencing ability.

EQUIPMENT

Rubber ball and five hoops.

CHALLENGES

1) Jump from hoop to hoop while carrying a ball. Dribble the ball five times in each hoop.

2) (For students lacking in hand-eye coordination, have them do this Challenge.) Jump from hoop to hoop while carrying a ball. Bounce and catch the ball five times in each hoop.

STRESS: *Soft* fingers on the ball dribble using a push, ***not*** a slap. Student jumps from one hoop to another, but stops in each hoop to perform the ball dribble or bounce and catch. Have the student verbalize (count out loud) when dribbling or bouncing and catching the ball.

SCOOTER BOARD WITH OBSTACLES

PERFORMANCE OBJECTIVES
By propelling a scooter board around obstacles without touching them, student demonstrates balance, gross-motor coordination, laterality, directionality and space awareness.

EQUIPMENT
Scooter board and two traffic cones.

CHALLENGES
1) Get in a prone position (get on your stomach) on the scooter board and use your hands and the strength of your arms to propel the scooter board between and around the cone obstacles.

2) (If time allows, do this Challenge.) Get on the scooter board again but this time get in a kneeling position (get down on your knees) on the scooter board and use your hands and the strength of your arms to propel yourself around and between the cone obstacles.

STRESS: Student starts in a good balanced position on the scooter board to begin the task. A definite pattern is followed without bumping into the obstacles. Student should attempt to use an alternate arm action in propelling the scooter board.

REBOUND NET AND LAUNCHING BOARD

PERFORMANCE OBJECTIVES
By catching a thrown bean bag on the rebound or a launched bean bag with varieties of dexterity, student demonstrates laterality and hand-eye coordination.

Teachers are encouraged to use the rebound net and launching board at least once a week as a 4th Station throughout the rest of the Program. It can be self-directed by the students.

LOW AND HIGH WALKING BOARDS

PERFORMANCE OBJECTIVES
By bouncing and catching a ball while walking a walking board, student demonstrates dynamic balance, hand-eye coordination, laterality and tactile awareness.

EQUIPMENT
High or intermediate and low walking boards, rubber ball, two bean bags and mats.

CHALLENGES
1) *HIGH OR INTERMEDIATE BOARD* - (Students who have not been on the high board previously should practice walking slowly forward with good body alignment. Students who are able to comfortably maneuver on the high board walking forward should be challenged to review walking forward and carrying a bean bag on top of each hand. Students not ready for the high board should be allowed to practice on the low board or intermediate board.)

2) *LOW BOARD* - Walk forward to the middle of the low board while carrying a ball. Bounce and catch the ball on alternate sides of the board (bounce and catch the ball on one side, then the other), then continue walking to the end of the low board.

STRESS: *LOW BOARD* - Student stops at the middle of the low board and carefully bounces the ball on the floor. Have the student bounce the ball on alternate sides of the board and verbalize (say out loud) *right* or *left*.

MAT STUNTS

PERFORMANCE OBJECTIVES
By performing a curl-up with body control, student demonstrates body image, kinesthetic awareness and abdominal strength.

EQUIPMENT

Mats and bean bag.

CHALLENGES

1) *REVIEW: CRAB WALK* - Lie on your back and push your body up into the air with your hands and feet. Remember to keep your body level. That is, your hips should not be any higher than your shoulders. Do it all again but this time place a bean bag on your stomach and push yourself up without letting the bean bag fall off.

2) *CURL-UP* - Lay down on your back and keep your body straight with your hands down along your sides and your legs together. When I say *Up*, slowly sit up. As you do so, bring your knees up too and grab them with your arms. Stay in this position as I say *Hold*. When I say *Down*, slowly release your knees and lay back down with your body straight again. (Instructor gives verbal cues of: *Up*, *Hold*, and *Down*. Allow 5 to 10 repetitions.)

STRESS: *CURL-UP* - Hands are *not* used to push off from the mat. Arms and legs start movement at the same time.

COORDINATION LADDER

> ### PERFORMANCE OBJECTIVES
> *By responding to a series of body support challenges on the coordination ladder, student demonstrates body awareness, laterality, dynamic balance and creativity.*

EQUIPMENT
 Coordination ladder.

CHALLENGES
 1) Can you travel down the coordination ladder using only two body parts?
 2) Can you move on the ladder using just three body parts?
 3) How would you move down the ladder using four body parts?

STRESS: Student creates own pattern of movement and attempts different types of movement when responding to the verbal problem posed.

REBOUNDER

PERFORMANCE OBJECTIVES
By feeling a number transcribed down the student's back and rebounding on a rebounder the same number of times as the number transcribed, student demonstrates tactile perception and locomotor control.

EQUIPMENT

Rebounder and mats.

CHALLENGES

1) *REVIEW: BODY AWARENESS REBOUNDING* - Rebound (jump) on the rebounder without losing control. Touch the body part that I call out as you rebound: head, shoulders, knees, (etc.). When I say *freeze*, stop rebounding without losing control.

2) *TACTILE REBOUNDING* - Stand on the rebounder. I will use my finger to write a number on your back. After I write the number, rebound (jump) the same number of times as the number I wrote on your back.

STRESS: Student positions body over the center area of the rebounder with feet shoulder distance apart ready to begin the challenge. Student rebounds with the body straight, head up, and eyes looking straight ahead, not down at his or her feet. *REMINDER* - Unbalanced landings or takeoffs are a key factor in the loss of body control.

CRISSCROSS ROPE WALKING WITH BALL BOUNCING

PERFORMANCE OBJECTIVES
By walking a crisscross pattern across a rope and bouncing a ball at the same time, student demonstrates laterality, directionality, balance hand-eye and foot-eye coordination.

EQUIPMENT
Ball 7" diameter, long rope and two bike tires.

CHALLENGES
1) Stand in one of the bicycle tires with a ball in your hands. Walk forward the length of the rope to the other bike tire. When walking forward, use a crossover step back and forth along the length of the rope and bounce the ball one time after each step you take. For example, cross your right leg over in front of your left leg and put your right foot down on the left side of the rope and bounce the ball once on the left side of the rope. Then continue ahead by bringing your left leg out from behind your right foot and crossing it over in front of your right leg and put your left foot down on the right side of the rope and bounce the ball once on the right side of the rope. Continue down the length of the rope by repeating your crossover steps and bouncing the ball one time after each step.

2) If you can successfully do the crossover step down the length of the rope while bouncing a ball, try it again, but this time *toss* the ball in the air and catch it once after each crossover step.

STRESS: Ball is bounced on the side of the rope where the forward foot is placed. Student starts in one tire and finishes in the opposite tire.

JUMP BOX

PERFORMANCE OBJECTIVES
By performing a forward roll after jumping and landing from a height,
student demonstrates dynamic balance, gross-motor coordination and body awareness.

EQUIPMENT
Jump box with incline board, red bike tire and mats.

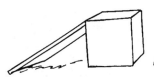 

CHALLENGES

1) Walk up the incline board and place your feet in the correct jumping position on the jump box. Jump into the *red* tire and land standing up with full body control. Then place your hands on the mat outside of the tire and do a *forward roll*. That is, get in a squat position by sitting on your heels with your hands flat on the mat outside of the tire and your knees together inside of your arms. Now tuck your chin against your knees, then raise your hips up high, push with your toes, lower the back of your head to the mat and roll over while keeping tucked in a round position like a ball.

2) This time, carefully *run* up the incline board and perform the same tasks as you did before.

STRESS: Bending of knees upon landing to cushion the body. Feet are in the tire and hands are placed outside of the tire on the *forward roll*. Hips raise up and guide the body over on the roll with the head coming under the body in a tucked position. (If the students experience difficulty with the tire, have them do a forward roll without it.)

LOW AND HIGH WALKING BOARDS

PERFORMANCE OBJECTIVES
By walking a walking board, stepping over two cross bars and bouncing a ball into a target, student demonstrates dynamic balance, laterality, visual-motor control and hand-eye coordination.

EQUIPMENT
High or intermediate and low walking boards, 7" diameter ball, bike tire, two cross bars and mats.

CHALLENGES
1) *REVIEW: HIGH OR INTERMEDIATE BOARD* - Walk forward to the middle of the high (or intermediate) board carrying the ball. Stop in the middle of the board and bounce the ball on alternate sides of the board. That is, bounce the ball once and catch it on one side and bounce the ball once and catch it on the other side. Afterwards, continue walking to the end of the board.

2) *LOW BOARD* - Walk forward carrying the ball. Step over the cross bar. Continue on to the middle of the low board. Stop in the middle, bounce and catch the ball once in each of the tires placed on both sides of the board. Then continue on and step over the second cross bar.

STRESS: *LOW BOARD* - Shifting of visual focusing as the student walks the board from the first cross bar to between the tire on the left and the tire on the right and on to the second cross bar and not looking down at feet.

MAT STUNTS

PERFORMANCE OBJECTIVES
By walking on hands and feet (seal walk), student demonstrates laterality, upper body strength, gross-motor coordination and body image.

EQUIPMENT
Mats.

CHALLENGES
1) *REVIEW: CURL-UP* - Lay down on your back and keep your body straight with your hands down along your sides and your legs together. When I say *Up*, slowly sit up. As you bend forward at the waist, bring your knees up too and grab them with your arms. Stay in this position as I say *Hold*. When I say *Down*, slowly release your knees and lay back down with your body straight again. (Instructor gives verbal cues of *Up*, *Hold*, and *Down*. Allow 5 to 10 repetitions.)

2) *SEAL WALK* - Get on your hands and knees. Extend your legs out behind you with your hands placed flat on the mat under your shoulders, arms straight and elbows stiff. Your weight is on your hands and on the top of your toes and feet. Walk forward on your hands with your legs straight, your toes dragging behind and your body swaying from side to side.

STRESS: *SEAL WALK* - Knees and legs (and or shins) do not drag on the mat, just the toes. Hands are flat on the mat and pointed out toward the sides of the body.

JUMPING PATTERNS WITH OBSTACLES

PERFORMANCE OBJECTIVES
By jumping through a series of obstacles, student demonstrates loco-motor control, foot-eye coordination, space awareness and motor planning ability.

EQUIPMENT
Two cross bars, six bike tires with two of them red and seven hoops.

CHALLENGES

1) *PATTERN 1* - Start from one end of the cross bar tire pat-tern. Jump into the first tire. Jump over the cross bar and into the red tire and freeze. Then perform a ***straddle jump*** into the two tires side by side. Make sure you land with one foot in one tire and the other foot in the other tire. Then jump into the tire in front of the 2nd cross bar. Jump over the cross bar and into the ***red*** tire and ***freeze***. Then jump out of the ***red*** tire. Remember to always ***freeze*** in place when you land in a ***red*** tire before you continue on. (If you run the students through the pattern more than once, choose different tires to be ***red***.)

2) *PATTERN 2* - Jump through the hoop pattern. Remember to use a ***straddle jump*** when two hoops are side by side. Move through the pattern again, but this time find a different way to move through it. (Each time you have them move through the pat-tern, challenge them to move through it differently.)

STRESS: Bending of knees on the takeoff and landing. *No* flatfooted landings. Arms help to lift the body. On *PATTERN 2*, tires may be used in place of hoops. (And vice versa for *PATTERN 1*.)

SCOOTER BOARD WITH OBSTACLES

PERFORMANCE OBJECTIVES
By propelling a scooter board between, under, and around obstacles, student demonstrates space awareness, gross-motor coordination, laterality, directionality and body awareness.

EQUIPMENT

Scooter board, two cross bars and one traffic cone.

CHALLENGES

Get in a prone position on the scooter board (lay on your stomach) and use your hands and the strength of your arms to propel the scooter board between and under and around the traffic cone obstacles.

STRESS: Student attempts to move through the cross bar and cone pattern without touching them.

REBOUNDER

PERFORMANCE OBJECTIVES
By listening to or viewing a math problem and then rebounding the number of times which correctly answers the problem, student demonstrates beginning numerical skills and locomotor control.

EQUIPMENT
 Rebounder, math number cards, and mats.

CHALLENGES
1) *REVIEW: TACTILE REBOUNDING* - Feel the numbers I write on your back and rebound (jump) the same number of times as the numbers I write.
2) *NUMBERS REBOUNDING* - I will tell you a math problem, you must rebound the same number of times as the number in the answer. Listen carefully! (Examples: 3 + 2 = , 5 - 3 = , etc.) Now I will hold up a card with a math problem on it. You must rebound the answer to the problem. (Example: 2 + 2 = ___ , etc.)

STRESS: Student takes good starting position over the center area of the rebounder. Student must listen and think before rebounding. Eyes look straight ahead. Arms help to maintain balance.

BASKET SHOOTING

PERFORMANCE OBJECTIVES
By shooting a ball into a waste basket, student demonstrates hand-eye coordination, directionality and laterality.

EQUIPMENT
Two waste paper baskets, two bike tires and two balls.

CHALLENGES

(Use two waste paper baskets and two 7" rubber balls. —It's best to have paper or cloth in the bottom of the baskets to cushion the ball. Organize two groups with one group shooting at each basket.)

1) Shoot the ball into the basket any way you want as you stand in the tire. You get three trials (turns). (Place the basket five to ten feet away from the tire depending on the ability of the students.)

2) Try shooting baskets again from the tire. But this time throw the ball underhand with your two hands. You get three trials.

3) Try shooting baskets again from the tire. But this time throw the ball overhand with your two hands, if you can. You get three trials. (Some students may not have the coordination for overhand throwing.)

STRESS: Bending of knees to begin the shooting motion and follow through of the arms toward the target after the release of the ball. Eyes focusing on target.

LOW AND HIGH WALKING BOARDS

PERFORMANCE OBJECTIVES
By maneuvering on the walking board and simultaneously bouncing and catching a ball, student demonstrates balance, laterality and hand-eye coordination.

EQUIPMENT
High or intermediate and low walking boards, two cross bars, two bike tires, 7" ball and mats.

CHALLENGES
1) *REVIEW: HIGH OR INTERMEDIATE BOARD* - Walk forward carrying the ball. Step over the cross bar. Continue on to the middle of the board. Stop in the middle, bounce and catch the ball once in each of the tires placed on both sides of the board. Then continue on and step over the second cross bar.
2) *LOW BOARD* - Walk forward two steps carrying the ball. Then bounce and catch the ball and move forward two more steps and bounce and catch the ball. Continue on in this manner until you reach the end of the low board.

STRESS: *LOW BOARD* - Pushing the ball down to bounce it on the floor, not just dropping the ball. Eyes focusing on the ball!

MAT STUNTS

PERFORMANCE OBJECTIVES
By elevating body upward with hands from a sitting position (elevator), student demonstrates body image, kinesthesis and upper body strength.

EQUIPMENT
   Mats.

CHALLENGES
   1) *REVIEW: SEAL WALK* - Get on your hands and knees. Extend your legs out behind you with your hands placed flat on the mat under your shoulders, arms straight and elbows stiff. Your weight is on your hands and on the top of your toes and feet. Walk forward on your hands with your legs straight, your toes dragging behind and your body swaying from side to side.
   2) *ELEVATOR* - Sit on the mat with your legs extended out straight and your hands on the mat under your shoulders. When I say *Level 1*, push against the mat with your hands and slowly elevate your trunk and legs up off the mat. When I say, *Level 2*, push yourself higher. When I say, *Level 3*, or *Top Floor*, push yourself to the highest point you can. Remember to support your weight on your hands and feet and keep your legs straight at all times.

STRESS: *ELEVATOR* - Knees do not bend as the body is elevated. At Level 3 (*Top Floor*) the body should be completely extended and straight from head to heels.

JUMP BOX

PERFORMANCE OBJECTIVES
By jumping from the jump box and performing a series of hand and finger actions in midair, student demonstrates sensory awareness, dynamic balance and agility.

EQUIPMENT
Jump box with incline board and mats.

CHALLENGES
1) Walk up the incline board, take a good position on the jump box, jump forward and:
   a) Clap your hands over your head and land on the mat with good balance.
   b) Snap your fingers above your head and land on the mat.
   c) Slap your knees and land on the mat.
2) Do it all again but this time carefully run up the incline board.

STRESS: Student attempts to get arms back down near the sides of his or her body (after hand clapping, knee slapping, etc.) to help accomplish a controlled landing.

COORDINATION LADDER

PERFORMANCE OBJECTIVES
By moving up the rungs and side rails of an inclined ladder, student demonstrates dynamic balance, foot-eye coordination, and space awareness.

EQUIPMENT
Coordination ladder, two intermediate walking board supports and mats.

CHALLENGES
(For the following challenges attach two intermediate walking board supports under the end rung of the coordination ladder in order to place the ladder in an incline position.)

1) Walk forward on the rungs of the coordination ladder until you reach the end supports, then turn and walk forward back to your starting position.

2) Walk forward on your hands and feet (four-legged position) by placing your hands on the side rails and your feet on the rungs. When you reach the end supports, turn and walk forward back to your starting position.

STRESS: Slow movements with complete body control. Feet placed on the rungs of the ladder, *not* the sides.

REBOUNDER

PERFORMANCE OBJECTIVES
By performing quarter turns while rebounding on a rebounder,
student demonstrates directionality, body awareness, and dynamic balance.

EQUIPMENT
Rebounder, number cards, and mats.

CHALLENGES
1) *REVIEW: NUMBERS REBOUNDING* - I will tell you a math problem, you must rebound the same number of times as the number in the answer. Listen carefully! (Examples: 3 + 2 = , 5 - 3 = , etc.) Now I will hold up a card with a math problem on it. You must rebound the answer to the problem. (Example: 2 + 2 = , etc.)

2) *QUARTER TURNS* - Rebound two times and then turn (twist) your body a ***quarter turn*** to the right. As you do so, say a rhythmic count: ***1—2—turn*** (***one*** for one rebound, ***two*** for two rebounds and ***turn*** for a ***quarter turn***). Keep rebounding and performing a ***quarter turn*** each time as you say your rhythmic count until you return back to your starting position on the rebounder.

STRESS: *QUARTER TURNS* - Four ***quarter turns*** will return the student to the starting position. Arms help to turn the body. All turns take place in midair over the center of the rebounder. Student does not look down at feet. Note: Teacher may wish to help ***cue*** the performer by verbalizing the rhythmic count of ***1—2—turn***, etc.

ANIMAL MOVEMENTS WITH OBSTACLES

PERFORMANCE OBJECTIVES
By frog jumping over and alligator crawling under obstacles, student demonstrates laterality, directionality, space awareness and kinesthetic awareness.

EQUIPMENT

Mats and two cross bars.

CHALLENGES

1) *FROG JUMP* - Squat and place your hands flat on the mat inside of your legs. Push from your toes and spring from the mat with your hands leaving the mat slightly ahead of your feet. Land in a squat position on your feet. Keep *frog jumping* down the mats and *frog jump* over the two cross bars on the mats.

2) *ALLIGATOR CRAWL* - Crawl on your stomach (*alligator crawl*) using bent arms and legs to move your body under the two cross bars on the mats.

STRESS: *FROG JUMP* - Student must motor plan *frog jump* movements so that the body lands the proper distance from the cross bar enabling a successful frog jump over the bar. Cross bars should be placed at different heights.

LOW AND HIGH WALKING BOARDS

PERFORMANCE OBJECTIVES
By walking across a walking board and bouncing and catching a ball in four tire targets, student demonstrates balance, laterality, directionality and hand-eye coordination.

EQUIPMENT
High or intermediate walking boards, 7" ball, four bike tires, low walking board and mats.

CHALLENGES
1) *REVIEW: HIGH OR INTERMEDIATE BOARD* - Walk forward two steps carrying the ball. Then bounce and catch the ball and move forward two more steps and bounce and catch the ball. Continue in this manner until you reach the end of the low board.
2) *LOW BOARD* - Walk forward carrying the ball, as you do so, bounce and catch the ball in the first tire on your left, then the first tire on your right, then the second tire on your left and finally the second tire on your right.

STRESS: *LOW BOARD* - Toes pointed forward while maneuvering on the board. (Feet do not turn sideward as the ball is bounced in the tires.) Best to have the student verbalize (say out loud) ***left*** or ***right*** as the ball is bounced in the tire.

MAT STUNTS

PERFORMANCE OBJECTIVES

By performing inchworm walk on hands and feet, student demonstrates body awareness, tactile and kinesthetic awareness, upper body strength and gross-motor coordination.

EQUIPMENT

Mats.

CHALLENGES

1) *REVIEW: ELEVATOR* - Sit on the mat with your legs extended out straight and your hands on the mat under your shoulders. When I say *Level 1*, push against the mat with your hands and slowly elevate your trunk and legs up off the mat. When I say, *Level 2*, push yourself higher. When I say, *Level 3*, or *Top Floor*, push yourself to the highest point you can. Remember to support your weight on your hands and feet and keep your legs straight at all times.

2) *INCHWORM* - Lay flat on your stomach on the mat. Keep your legs straight and push your body up with your hands and arms so that all your weight is supported on your hands and toes (push-up position). Keep your hands stationary (don't move them) and walk your feet forward towards your hands by taking short steps and keeping your legs straight. When your feet get as close to your hands as they can comfortably get without bending your knees, start moving your hands forward in short steps while you keep your feet stationary (in one place). When your body is back to your starting position, move your feet up again, then your hands forward in the same manner as you did before. Continue this pattern until you reach the edge of the mats.

STRESS: *INCHWORM* - Hands are stationary with the arms and the legs are straight as the feet move forward, and the feet are stationary with the legs and the arms are straight as the hands move forward.

HOPPING PATTERN WITH HOOPS AND ROPES

PERFORMANCE OBJECTIVES
By hopping on either foot within the spaces provided by the hoops and ropes, student demonstrates balance, locomotor coordination, laterality and space awareness.

EQUIPMENT
Long rope, four jump ropes and six hoops.

CHALLENGES

1) *PATTERN 1* - On your preferred foot hop into the first space in the first hoop, hop into the 2nd space of the first hoop, hop into the first space of the 2nd hoop, hop into the second space of the 2nd hoop, hop into the first space of the 3rd hoop, hop into the 2nd space of the 3rd hoop, and finally, hop out of the 3rd hoop. Do it all again, but this time hop on your other foot.

2) *PATTERN 2* - On your preferred foot, hop into the right space of the first hoop, hop sideward into the left space of the first hoop, hop forward into the left space of the 2nd hoop, hop sideward into the right space of the 2nd hoop, hop sideward into the left space of the 2nd hoop, hop forward into the left space of the 3rd hoop, hop sideward into the right space of the 3rd hoop, hop sideward into the left space of the 3rd hoop, and finally, hop forward out of the 3rd hoop. Do it all again, but this time hop on your other foot.

STRESS: Balance maintained on one foot with soft, light movements. Shoulders back. (Ropes are placed *under* the hoops as illustrated for *PATTERNS 1 and 2*.)

JUMP BOX

PERFORMANCE OBJECTIVES
By moving through a series of obstacles in a designated manner, student demonstrates locomotor coordination, dynamic balance, body and space awareness and directionality.

EQUIPMENT
Jump box with incline board, bike tire, two cross bars and mats.

CHALLENGES
1) Walk up the incline board and jump from the jump box and land in the tire.
2) Perform a ***forward roll*** over the first cross bar. For those of you who have forgotten, perform a ***forward roll*** by starting in a squat position by sitting on your heels with your hands flat on the mat and your knees together inside of your arms. Now tuck your chin against your knees, then raise your hips up high, push with your toes, lower the back of your head to the mat and roll over while keeping tucked in a round position like a ball.
3) Crawl under the second cross bar.

STRESS: Proper hand placement and tucking of head on the ***forward roll***. Cross bar is placed close to the tire so that the ***roll*** can be accomplished with feet starting from inside the tire.

SCOOTER BOARD

PERFORMANCE OBJECTIVES
By pulling on a rope while lying on a scooter board, student demon-strates tactile and kinesthetic awareness, arm strength, balance and laterality.

EQUIPMENT

Scooter board and a long rope.

CHALLENGES

(For the following challenge, tie two short jump ropes together or use one long rope. Instructor or aide should hold one end of the rope.)

Get in a prone position (on your stomach) on the scooter board and grip the rope at the opposite end from the instructor. Pull yourself toward the instructor by using a ***hand over hand grip*** on the rope (one hand grips the rope then the other hand grips the rope ahead of the other hand and so on).

STRESS: Firm grip on the rope by both the instructor and student. Feet do not touch the floor. Rope goes under the scooter board and between the wheels.

REBOUNDER

PERFORMANCE OBJECTIVES
*By performing half turns while rebounding on a rebounder,
student demonstrates directionality, body awareness, and dynamic balance.*

EQUIPMENT
Rebounder and mats.

CHALLENGES
1) *REVIEW: QUARTER TURNS* - Rebound two times and then turn (twist) your body a *quarter turn* to the right. As you do so, say a rhythmic count: *1—2—turn* (*one* for one rebound, *two* for two rebounds and *turn* for a *quarter turn*). Keep rebounding and performing a *quarter turn* each time as you say your rhythmic count until you return back to your starting position on the rebounder.

2) *HALF TURNS* - Rebound two times and then turn (twist) your body one *half turn* to the right so that you land facing in the opposite direction. Continue to rebound two more times and then do another *half turn* to the right to bring yourself back to your original starting position. Just as you did with *quarter turns*, say a rhythmic count as you rebound and turn. Try to keep your rhythmic pattern throughout both turns and rebounds.

STRESS: Turn or twist the body at the height of the rebound. Keep feet a shoulder's distance apart and over the center area of the rebounder. *Do not* watch feet! Teacher may wish to "*cue*" the performer at first by verbalizing the rhythmic count of *1—2—turn*, etc.

LOW AND HIGH WALKING BOARDS

PERFORMANCE OBJECTIVES
By balancing like a swan on the left and then the right foot in the tire targets on a walking board, student demonstrates static balance, spatial orientation and unilateral control.

EQUIPMENT
High or intermediate and low walking boards, six bike tires, 7" ball and mats.

CHALLENGES
1) *REVIEW: HIGH OR INTERMEDIATE BOARD* - Walk forward carrying the ball, as you do so, bounce and catch the ball in the first tire on your left, then the first tire on your right, then the second tire on your left and finally the second tire on your right.

2) *LOW BOARD* - Walk forward and perform a *swan balance* on your left foot in the first tire. Continue walking and perform a *swan balance* on your right foot in the second tire. When performing a *swan balance*, balance on one foot only, bend forward at the waist and extend your arms out sideward.

STRESS: LOW BOARD - Emphasize how they are to perform a *swan balance*.

MAT STUNTS

PERFORMANCE OBJECTIVES
By quickly changing body positions on signal from the
teacher, student demonstrates body image and control, agility and laterality.

EQUIPMENT
  Mats.

CHALLENGES
  1) *REVIEW: INCHWORM* - Lay flat on your stomach on the mat. Keep your legs straight and push your body up with your hands and arms so that all your weight is supported on your hands and toes (push-up position). Keep your hands stationary (don't move them) and walk your feet forward towards your hands by taking short steps and keeping your legs straight. When your feet get as close to your hands as they can comfortably get without bending your knees, start moving your hands forward in short steps while you keep your feet stationary (in one place). When your body is back to your starting position, move your feet up again, then your hands forward in the same manner as you did before. Continue this pattern until you reach the edge of the mats.
  2) *BODY AWARENESS REACTION DRILL* - Quickly change body positions on the mat when I call out these challenges: ***front*** (get on your stomach), ***back***, ***left side***, ***right side***, ***feet***, ***seat***, ***knees***, (etc.).

STRESS: *BODY AWARENESS REACTION DRILL* - Quick movements, but students do not ***throw*** themselves onto the mat. ***Do not*** call ***knee*** position when the students are standing because tendency is to drop onto the knees.

MOVEMENT PATTERN WITH TIRES AND ROPES

PERFORMANCE OBJECTIVES

By jumping and hopping into tires, and by jumping and hopping over ropes and walking backwards on ropes, student demonstrates locomotor skill and coordination, dynamic balance and spatial orientation.

EQUIPMENT

Four bike tires and three jump ropes.

CHALLENGES

1) Start inside the first tire, then jump back and forth over the rope until you reach the inside of the second tire.

2) From the second tire, perform a backwards *balance walk* on the rope to the third tire. Remember to walk on the rope not on the floor beside it.

3) From the inside the third tire, hop forwards back and forth over the rope until you're inside the fourth tire.

4) (If time allows after several repetitions, ask the students to show you a different way of going through the pattern.)

STRESS: Controlled movement—not speed, and getting both feet off the floor at the same time on the jumping pattern.

COORDINATION LADDER

PERFORMANCE OBJECTIVES
By moving across the ladder in various ways, student demonstrates dynamic balance, locomotor coordination, space awareness, foot-eye coordination and motor planning ability.

EQUIPMENT
Coordination ladder and a mat.

CHALLENGES
1) Hop between rungs of the coordination ladder.
2) ***Crab walk*** on the sides or rungs of the ladder. (Remember, you perform a ***crab walk*** by starting with your body in an inverted position. That is, lie on your back and push your hips and back up into the air with your feet and hands. Make sure your weight is distributed evenly on your feet and hands. That is, don't push any harder on your feet than you do on your hands and don't let your hips get higher than your shoulders. Start moving in the direction of your head or feet.)
3) Show me a different way of getting to the end of the ladder. (Have them do several creative challenges like this.)

STRESS: Arms help to lift the body on the hop. Student concentrates on the ***control*** of movement not speed.

SCOOTER BOARD

PERFORMANCE OBJECTIVES
By propelling a scooter board while "walking" on hands, student demonstrates laterality, body awareness, upper body strength and gross-motor coordination.

EQUIPMENT

Scooter board and traffic cone.

CHALLENGES

1) Walk on your hands with your legs extended and your feet resting on the scooter board. Direct your body around the traffic cone obstacle.
2) (If time allows, have students do this challenge.) Choose your own way to get on the scooter board. Then move backwards on the scooter board around the cone obstacle.

STRESS: Body kept straight with the elbows stiff, similar to a ***seal walk***.

JUMP BOX

PERFORMANCE OBJECTIVES
By jumping from a jump box and grabbing the ball in midair, student demonstrates dynamic balance, hand-eye coordination, body awareness and agility.

EQUIPMENT
Jump box with incline board, 7" ball and mats.

CHALLENGES

1) Walk up the incline board and take the correct jumping position on the jump box. Jump from the box and grab the ball I'm holding in front of the jump box. Then land with the ball clutched in both hands. (Ball is held in one hand extended out in front of the jumper. Student grabs the ball held *stationary* by the instructor. Ball must be held at a level and distance where the student must jump out *and up* to reach the ball.)

2) Walk up the incline board and jump off the jump box again. But this time, click your heels together in midair instead of grabbing the ball.

3) Do it again, but this time carefully *run* up the incline board.

STRESS: *1)* - Student focuses on the ball and attempts to grasp the ball at the height of the jump. *2)* - Student attempts to get arms back down near the sides of his or her body after clicking heels to help accomplish a controlled landing. Heels are clicked together at the height of the jump.

LOW AND HIGH WALKING BOARDS

PERFORMANCE OBJECTIVES
*By walking a walking board and focusing on a moving target,
student demonstrates dynamic balance, ocular pursuit and laterality.*

EQUIPMENT
High or intermediate and low walking boards, two bike tires, small ball with attached cord and mats.

CHALLENGES

1) *REVIEW: HIGH OR INTERMEDIATE BOARD* - Walk forward on the board and perform a *swan balance* in each of the two tires placed on the board. In the first tire perform a *swan balance* on your left foot and in the second tire perform it on your right foot. When performing a *swan balance*, balance on one foot only, bend forward at the waist and extend your arms out sideward.

2) *LOW BOARD* - Walk forward and keep your eyes glued to the swinging ball. (Ball is held at eye level at the end of the board. Use a styrofoam or plastic ball suspended by a string or cord. Ball is swung slowly from side to side.)

STRESS: *LOW BOARD* - Head ***does not*** move from side to side when tracking the ball. The eyes should follow the movement of the ball without any head movement.

MAT STUNTS

PERFORMANCE OBJECTIVES
By performing a series of rabbit hops and forward rolls in sequence, student demonstrates memory sequencing and motor planning ability, gross-motor coordination, body awareness and laterality.

EQUIPMENT
Mats.

CHALLENGES
1) *REVIEW: BODY AWARENESS REACTION DRILL* - Quickly change body positions on the mat when I call out these challenges: **front** (get on your stomach), **back**, **left side**, **right side**, **feet**, **seat**, **knees**, (etc.).

2) *RABBIT HOP FORWARD ROLL COMBINATION* - Perform a **rabbit hop** followed by a **forward roll**. Keep this same pattern until you reach the end of the mat. For a **rabbit hop**, remember to squat down with your hands placed flat on the mat and your knees together between your arms. Now reach forward with your hands and jump your feet up to your hands. For a **forward roll**, remember to start in a squat position by sitting on your heels with your hands flat on the mat and your knees together inside of your arms just like the starting position of the rabbit hop. Now tuck your chin against your knees, then raise your hips up high, push with your toes, lower the back of your head to the mat and roll over while keeping tucked in a round position like a ball.

STRESS: *RABBIT HOP FORWARD ROLL COMBINATION* - Good starting position (sitting on the heels with the knees together inside of the arms) for both the **rabbit hop** and the **forward roll**. Student takes time and thinks through each movement.

HOPPING PATTERN WITH TIRES, ROPES AND HOOPS

PERFORMANCE OBJECTIVES
By hopping and jumping through a series of obstacles, student demonstrates locomotor coordination, balance, spatial orientation, laterality and foot-eye coordination.

EQUIPMENT
Cross bar, four bike tires and two jump ropes.

CHALLENGES
1) Starting inside of the first tire, *hop* back and forth over the rope on your right foot until you reach the second tire.
2) From inside the second tire, *jump* over the cross bar and land inside the third tire.
3) From inside the third tire, *hop* back and forth over the rope on your *left* foot until you reach the final tire.

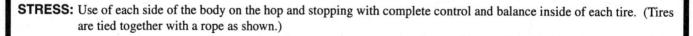

STRESS: Use of each side of the body on the hop and stopping with complete control and balance inside of each tire. (Tires are tied together with a rope as shown.)

COORDINATION LADDER WITH JUMP BOX

PERFORMANCE OBJECTIVES
By climbing a ladder and jumping into specific tire targets, student demonstrates dynamic balance, gross-motor coordination and space awareness.

EQUIPMENT

Jump box with coordination ladder, three bike tires and mats.

CHALLENGES

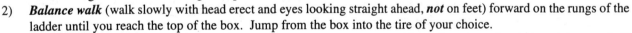

1) Walk forward on your hands and feet (the four-legged position) on the rungs of the ladder until you reach the top of the box. Stand up and jump from the box into the tire of your choice (three tires as targets). Emphasize landing with complete body control. (Note: Ladder is attached to the top of the jump box for all challenges. It should fit firmly in place with the end rung of the ladder resting on top of the box.)

2) *Balance walk* (walk slowly with head erect and eyes looking straight ahead, *not* on feet) forward on the rungs of the ladder until you reach the top of the box. Jump from the box into the tire of your choice.

3) (Challenge the student to jump from the box in various ways such as sidewards, using a hand clap, doing one half turns, clicking heels, etc.)

STRESS: Slow movements with complete body control. Bending of knees on both the takeoff and the landing of the jump.

SCOOTER BOARD

PERFORMANCE OBJECTIVES
By transporting the body on a scooter board in a variety of ways around two obstacles, student demonstrates laterality, body awareness, directionality, balance and gross-motor coordination.

EQUIPMENT
Scooter board and two cones.

CHALLENGES
1) Sit on the scooter board and transport your body using only your feet.
2) Kneel on the scooter board, lean forward with your weight on your hands and transport your body using your hands.
3) (Do Challenge #3 only if time is available.) Lie with your back on the scooter board, support your head with your hands and transport your body using only your feet.

STRESS: Good starting position on the scooter board. Student attempts to follow a directed pattern of movement in and around the cones in all of the challenges.

REBOUNDER

PERFORMANCE OBJECTIVES
By performing straddle jumps on a rebounder, student demonstrates body awareness, bilateral control, and dynamic balance.

EQUIPMENT
Rebounder and mats.

CHALLENGES
1) *REVIEW: HALF TURNS* - Rebound two times and turn (twist) your body one **half turn** to the right on each rebound while in mid air so that you land facing in the opposite direction on the first rebound and return to your starting position on the second rebound. Do it again, but this time rebound and do **half turns** to the left. Now start rebounding again but do a **half turn** in the direction I call out: **left turn**, **right turn**, (etc.).

2) *STRADDLE JUMPS* - Start rebounding over the center of the rebounder with your feet close together. Keep your hands on your hips. Rebound once with your feet together then move them apart in mid air and land with your feet apart, rebound with them apart and land with them together and rebound with them together and so on. These are called **straddle jumps**. (Student does five to ten **straddle jumps**.)

STRESS: Keep head up and shoulders back maintaining good body alignment. Body position must be maintained over the center point of the rebounder. *STRADDLE JUMPS* - Both feet must move sideward and return at the same time. Practice on the floor before performing on the rebounder.

LOW AND HIGH WALKING BOARDS

PERFORMANCE OBJECTIVES
By performing a cat walk on the walking board, student demonstrates dynamic balance, laterality, kinesthetic and tactile awareness and gross-motor coordination.

EQUIPMENT
High or intermediate and low walking boards, small ball with attached cord and mats.

CHALLENGES
1) *REVIEW: HIGH OR INTERMEDIATE BOARD* - Walk forward and keep your eyes glued to the swinging ball. (Ball is held at eye level at the end of the board. Use a styrofoam or plastic ball suspended by a string or cord. Ball is swung slowly from side to side.)
2) *LOW BOARD* - Perform a *cat walk* moving forward as you balance on your hands and feet until you reach the end of the board. Note that a *cat walk* is almost the same as a *dog walk*. As you remember, when you do a *dog walk*, you walk on your hands and feet with your weight evenly distributed on your hands and feet. It's the same for a *cat walk* except you're walking on a beam and your hands or cat claws are grasping the sides of the beam.

STRESS: *REVIEW: HIGH OR INTERMEDIATE BOARD* - Eyes track the swinging ball without any head movement. *LOW BOARD* - Hands lead movement and stay out in front of the body.

MAT STUNTS

PERFORMANCE OBJECTIVES

By walking on hands with assistance as in the wheelbarrow walk, *student demonstrates body awareness, upper arm and shoulder strength, laterality and gross-motor coordination.*

EQUIPMENT

Mats.

CHALLENGES

1) *REVIEW: RABBIT HOP FORWARD ROLL COMBINATION* - Perform a **rabbit hop** followed by a **forward roll**. Keep this same pattern until you reach the end of the mat. For a **rabbit hop**, remember to squat down with your hands placed flat on the mat and your knees together between your arms. Now reach forward with your hands and jump your feet up to your hands. For a **forward roll**, remember to start in a squat position by sitting on your heels with your hands flat on the mat and your knees together inside of your arms just like the starting position of the rabbit hop. Now tuck your chin against your knees, then raise your hips up high, push with your toes, lower the back of your head to the mat and roll over while keeping tucked in a round position like a ball.

2) *WHEELBARROW WALK* - Find a partner. One partner gets down on hands and knees and the other one holds the legs of his or her partner between the ankles and the knees (**not** at the ankles) so that the legs are straight and off the floor. When you reach the end of the mats, partners change positions and **wheelbarrow walk** back to their starting point.

STRESS: *WHEELBARROW WALK* - Arms are kept straight and support the body weight. Hands are flat on the mat for a solid base of support.

OBSTACLE COURSE

PERFORMANCE OBJECTIVES
By responding to a series of challenges to transport one's self through an obstacle course, student demonstrates locomotor coordination, dynamic balance, body and space awareness, directionality and motor planning ability.

EQUIPMENT
Jump box with coordination ladder, red bike tire, two cross bars, car tire with support stand and mats.

CHALLENGES
1) Perform a *dog walk* up the inclined ladder to the top of the jump box. (Remember that a *dog walk* is a 4-legged walk with your weight distributed evenly on your hands and feet.)
2) Jump from the box into the red tire target.
3) Perform a *forward roll* over the first low cross bar. (Remember, you perform the *forward roll* by starting in a squat position by sitting on your heels with your hands flat on the mat and your knees together inside of your arms. Now tuck your chin against your knees, then raise your hips up high, push with your toes, lower the back of your head to the mat and roll over while keeping tucked in a round position like a ball.)
4) Crawl under the second low cross bar without touching the bar.
5) Go through the car tire without touching the tire.
6) (After several repetitions of the above tasks, challenge the students to find a different way of moving through the obstacles.)

STRESS: Land on the balls of the feet and low bending of the knees to cushion the landing in the tire. Hands are placed over the bar and close to the bar on the *forward roll* with the head coming under the body in a tucked position. (Obstacle course should be on mats.)

REBOUNDER

PERFORMANCE OBJECTIVES
By performing lateral jumps on a rebounder, student demonstrates body awareness, bilateral control, and dynamic balance.

EQUIPMENT
Rebounder and mats.

CHALLENGES
1) *REVIEW: STRADDLE JUMPS* - Start rebounding over the center of the rebounder with your feet close together. Keep your hands on your hips. Rebound once with your feet together then move them apart in mid air and land with your feet apart, rebound with them apart and land with them together and rebound with them together and so on. These are called **straddle jumps**.

2) *LATERAL JUMPS* - Stand in the center of the rebounder with your feet together. Hold your hands in a comfortable position to help balance your body when you jump. Start jumping (rebounding) in short sideward movements while keeping your feet and legs together. That is, make a short jump to the left, then to the right, then to the left, then to the right and so on.

STRESS: *LATERAL JUMPS* - Lateral jumps must be **spotted** very carefully. Student can easily lose control. Feet stay together and move as one unit in short sideward motions back and forth. Have the students practice on the floor before performing on the rebounder.

COORDINATION LADDER

PERFORMANCE OBJECTIVES
*By responding to a series of verbal challenges
on the coordination ladder, student demonstrates body and space awareness, dynamic balance, foot-eye coordination, motor planning ability and listening skills.*

EQUIPMENT
Coordination ladder and bean bag.

CHALLENGES
1) Show me how you can jump into every other space between the rungs of the ladder.
2) Can you walk on the rungs of the ladder balancing a bean bag on your head?
3) Find a way of moving from one end of the ladder to the other end that you have never used before.

STRESS: Listening skills and thinking before moving.

REBOUND NET AND LAUNCHING BOARD

PERFORMANCE OBJECTIVES
*By tossing and catching and launching and catching a bean bag in a variety
of ways, student demonstrates hand-eye and foot-eye coordination and tactile awareness.*

EQUIPMENT
Rebound net, launching board and classroom set of bean bags.

CHALLENGES
1) *REBOUND NET* - Throw a bean bag (or tennis ball) against the rebound net and perform the following tasks: a) Clap your hands and catch the bean bag. b) Snap your fingers and catch the bean bag. c) Slap your knees and catch the bean bag. d) Touch your toes and catch the bean bag. (This is a much more difficult task.)

2) *LAUNCHING BOARD* - (Students able to catch a bean bag in each hand individually should be challenged to launch and catch two bags.) Place two bean bags side by side across the launching board, not on top of each other. (Use two different colored bean bags, if available.) Stomp your foot on the other end of the launching board and catch the two bean bags. Catch the lowest bag first.

STRESS: *REBOUND NET* - Eyes watch (follow) the bean bag into the hands which move out to meet the bag. Hands must work together as a catching unit. Body positioning in front of the bean bag is important to success. *LAUNCHING BOARD* - Hands are cupped forming a pocket under the lowest bag first and then move to the second bag. More skillful students can try catching each bag with one hand.

LOW AND HIGH WALKING BOARDS

PERFORMANCE OBJECTIVES
By tossing and catching a ball with the teacher while maneuvering along a walking board, student demonstrates dynamic balance, tactile awareness and hand-eye coordination.

EQUIPMENT
High or intermediate and low walking boards, 7" ball and mats.

CHALLENGES
1) *REVIEW: HIGH OR INTERMEDIATE BOARD* - Perform a ***cat walk*** moving forward as you balance on your hands and feet until you reach the end of the board. Note that a ***cat walk*** is almost the same as a ***dog walk***. As you remember, when you do a ***dog walk***, you walk on your hands and feet with your weight evenly distributed on them. It's the same for a ***cat walk*** except you're walking on a beam and your hands or cat claws are grasping the sides of the beam.

2) *LOW BOARD* - Walk forward carrying a ball. As you walk forward with the ball, toss and catch it with me (instructor). Toss the ball three times underhand to me (instructor) and catch it from me (instructor) three times.

STRESS: *LOW BOARD* - Student tosses and catches the ball after every few steps. Eyes watch the ball!

MAT STUNTS

PERFORMANCE OBJECTIVES
By performing a series of modified push-ups, student demonstrates upper body strength, body awareness and kinesthetic awareness.

EQUIPMENT
Mats.

CHALLENGES
1) *REVIEW: WHEELBARROW WALK* - Find a partner. One partner gets down on hands and knees and the other one holds the legs of his or her partner between the ankles and the knees (*not* at the ankles) so that the legs are straight and off the floor. When you reach the end of the mats, partners change positions and *wheelbarrow walk* back to their starting point.

2) *MODIFIED PUSH-UPS* - Kneel down on the mat and place your hands flat on the mat under your shoulders with your arms extended straight and your feet held off the mat. Keep your body straight from your head to your knees in an inclined position. You perform a *modified push-up* by lowering your body until your chin or your chest touches the mat, and then by pushing your body back up to your starting position. Remember to keep your body straight and rigid from your head to your knees throughout the *modified push-up*. (Student attempts to do five to ten *modified push-ups* in succession.)

STRESS: *MODIFIED PUSH-UPS* - Body is kept straight, feet are held off the mat and the stomach area does *not* touch the mat when the body is lowered. Several students can perform together.

JUMPING PATTERN WITH ROPES AND TIRES

PERFORMANCE OBJECTIVES
By jumping through an obstacle course of ropes and tires, student demonstrates locomotor coordination, balance, space awareness, directionality and motor planning ability.

EQUIPMENT
Five jump ropes and six bike tires.

CHALLENGES

1) Jump through the rope and tire pattern. Jump forward over the rope into the tire. Jump sideward to the left over the rope into the tire. Jump forward over the rope into the tire. Jump sideward to the right over the rope into the tire. Jump forward over the rope into the tire. Jump sideward to the left over the rope into the tire. Jump forward over the rope and out of the pattern.

2) Do it all again, but this time twist in the air so you're facing in the direction of your next jump.

3) Do it all again, but this time move through the pattern in a different way.

STRESS: Bending of the knees on the takeoff and landing of each jump. Both feet leave the floor at the same time on each jump.

COORDINATION LADDER WITH JUMP BOX

PERFORMANCE OBJECTIVES
By moving through a series of obstacles combined with a coordination ladder and jump box, student demonstrates motor planning ability, dynamic balance and locomotor coordination.

EQUIPMENT
Jump box with coordination ladder, two bike tires, jump rope and mats.

CHALLENGES

1) *Creep* on your hands and knees up the rungs of the coordination ladder to the top of the jump box.

2) Jump from the jump box and perform a *one half turn* in midair so that you land in the tire facing the jump box.

3) Perform a *crisscross walk* or sometimes called a *scissors walk* moving backwards the length of the rope to the second tire. That is, cross your right foot over the rope behind you and put it behind your left foot, then swing your left foot out to the left and bring it behind your right foot and put it down across the rope behind you. Then swing your right foot out to the right and bring it behind your left foot and put it down across the rope behind you. And so on.

4) (After performing the first three activities in succession have the students perform activity #4.) Show me a different way of moving up the coordination ladder and down from the Jump box across the tire and rope pattern.

STRESS: Student jumps from the jump box and then twists or turns his or her body. Front foot moves first on the backwards *scissors walk*. Make sure the rope is tied between the two tires as shown.

SCOOTER BOARD

PERFORMANCE OBJECTIVES
By transporting the body on a scooter board through an obstacle course without touching obstacles, student demonstrates gross-motor coordination, balance, space awareness and directionality.

EQUIPMENT
Scooter board and two cross bars placed in a straight line as illustrated.

CHALLENGES
Lay down on your stomach on the scooter board. Use only your hands to move the scooter board under the first cross bar and under the second cross bar. Then come around to the other side of the second cross bar and move under it and then under the first first cross bar again to complete a figure eight pattern. Try to do it all without touching the cones or cross bars.

STRESS: Student attempts to go *under* the cross bars and *around* the cones without touching.

REBOUNDER

PERFORMANCE OBJECTIVES
*By performing jumping jacks on a rebounder, student
demonstrates bilateral control, body awareness, and dynamic balance.*

EQUIPMENT
Rebounder and mats.

CHALLENGES

1) *REVIEW: LATERAL JUMPS* - Stand in the center of the rebounder with your feet together. Hold your hands in a comfortable position to help balance your body when you jump. Start jumping (rebounding) in short sideward movements while keeping your feet and legs together. That is, make a short jump to the left, then to the right, then to the left, then to the right and so on.

2) *JUMPING JACKS* - Start with your feet together over the center of the rebounder with your arms down at your side. Rebound (jump) with your hands and arms moving out and up over your head as your feet move out sideward. While in this position, jump (rebound) again and move your hands, arms and feet back to their starting positions to complete one ***jumping jack***. (Student does five to ten ***jumping jacks***.)

STRESS: *JUMPING JACKS* - Arms and legs begin sideward movement and return to their starting positions at the same time. Hands may be clapped together over the head (optional). Have the students practice on the floor first. Practice can be in a small group formation.

LOW AND HIGH WALKING BOARDS

PERFORMANCE OBJECTIVES
By walking a walking board with eyes closed, student demonstrates dynamic balance, tactile and kinesthetic awareness.

EQUIPMENT
High or intermediate and low walking boards, 7" diameter ball, mats and a blindfold.

CHALLENGES
1) *REVIEW: HIGH OR INTERMEDIATE BOARD* - Walk forward carrying a ball. As you walk forward with the ball, toss and catch it with me (instructor). Toss the ball three times underhand to me (instructor) and catch it from me (instructor) three times.

2) *LOW BOARD* - Stand at one end of the low walking board. Close your eyes or I can put a blindfold on you so you can't see, whichever you prefer. Carefully walk forward with your eyes closed (or covered) and maintain your balance all the way to the end of the low walking board.

STRESS: *LOW BOARD* - Use of arms to make adjustments in balancing. Student carefully feels board with feet. ***Instructor should walk alongside of the student and offer help, if needed.***

MAT STUNTS

PERFORMANCE OBJECTIVES
By log rolling *across mats in various directions and holding a ball with the hands or feet, student demonstrates body and spatial awareness, laterality, tactile and kinesthetic awareness and agility.*

EQUIPMENT
Classroom set of balls and mats.

CHALLENGES
1) *REVIEW: MODIFIED PUSH-UPS* - (Six or more students can practice this stunt at the same time across the mats.) Kneel down on the mat and place your hands flat on the mat under your shoulders with your arms extended straight and your feet held off the mat. Keep your body straight from your head to your knees in an inclined position. You perform a ***modified push-up*** by lowering your body until your chin or your chest touches the mat, and then by pushing your body back up to your starting position. Remember to keep your body straight and rigid from your head to your knees throughout the ***modified push-up***. (Student attempts to do five to ten ***modified push-ups*** in succession.)

2) *DIRECTIONAL LOG ROLLS WITH BALL* - (Three or four students can perform this stunt at the same time.) Lay down across the mats on your backs with your arms extended beyond your heads and your bodies kept straight. Get ready for the following challenges where I will ask you to ***log roll*** (roll) to the right or left while holding one or more balls. When you ***log roll***, roll completely over and return to your starting position: a) Hold a ball between your hands and ***log roll*** to the right, to the left, to the right, (Etc.). b) Hold a ball firmly between your feet and log roll to the left, to the right, to the left, (etc.). c) Hold a ball between your hands and one between your feet. Roll to the right, to the left, (etc.). d) (For a variation on all challenges, challenge the students to do two rolls to the left, three to the right, etc.)

STRESS: *DIRECTIONAL LOG ROLLS WITH BALL* - The hips direct the movement with the body making a complete roll onto the stomach and over onto the back moving in the designated direction. (Student must be able to successfully process tactile and kinesthetic information so that constant awareness of body position in space and ball contact control is maintained.)

LONG JUMP PATTERN

PERFORMANCE OBJECTIVES
By jumping from one tire into another and landing with complete body control, student demonstrates locomotor coordination, kinesthesis, space awareness, directionality and motor planning ability.

EQUIPMENT
Two jump ropes and six bike tires.

CHALLENGES
1) (For this challenge, place the ropes parallel to each other so that all tires across the ropes from each other are an equal distance.) Start at one end of the *brook* and jump from inside the first tire across the *brook* into the next tire. Then jump into the tire closest to you on the same side. Then jump across the *brook* again into the tire directly across from you. Then jump into the tire next to you at the end of the *brook*. Finally, jump across the brook into the tire directly across from you.

2) (For this challenge, slightly angle the ropes forming the *brook* so that each jump across the *brook* becomes longer and requires a greater effort for success. See illustration.) Do it all again. Start at the narrow end of the *brook*. (Student starts at the narrow end of the *brook* and moves towards the wider end. Each jump across the *brook* requires new judgement and decision making.)

STRESS: Soft landing on the "balls" of the feet and stopping with full body control in each tire.

REBOUNDER

PERFORMANCE OBJECTIVES
By rebounding on a rebounder and catching a thrown ball, student demonstrates dynamic balance, body awareness, and hand-eye coordination.

EQUIPMENT
Rebounder, ball and mats.

CHALLENGES
1) *REVIEW: JUMPING JACKS* - Start with your feet together over the center of the rebounder with your arms down at your side. Rebound (jump) with your hands and arms moving out and up over your head as your feet move out sideward. While in this position, jump (rebound) again and move your hands, arms and feet back to their starting positions to complete one *jumping jack*. (Student does five to ten *jumping jacks*. Make sure arms and legs move in a coordinated rhythmic sequence.)
2) *REBOUNDING WITH BALL CATCHING* - Rebound over the center of the rebounder. While rebounding, catch the ball that I throw underhand to you and toss it back. Maintain your rebounding rhythm. (Student rebounds three to five times while catching and tossing the ball.)

STRESS: *REBOUNDING WITH BALL CATCHING* - Eyes watch the ball into the hands on the catching pattern. The hands must prepare properly to receive the ball. Student must be aware of maintaining the center position on the rebounder. Catch is made while the student is airborne. Proper timing on the ball toss by the teacher or aide is important for successful performance.

BALL DRIBBLING THROUGH HOOP PATTERN

PERFORMANCE OBJECTIVES
By dribbling a ball through a series of hoops, student demonstrates hand-eye coordination, spatial orientation and tactile awareness.

EQUIPMENT

Ball and four hoops.

CHALLENGES

Dribble the ball through the hoop pattern without touching the hoops with the ball or losing control of the ball. Be sure to use only one hand when you dribble. If you have difficulty dribbling the ball, bounce and catch the ball through the hoop pattern or do a little of both, whatever you are able to do.

STRESS: Using a push on the dribble with *soft fingers* and not a slapping motion. Fingers are spread and stay close to the ball.

JUMP BOX

PERFORMANCE OBJECTIVES
By moving up and down an incline board and coordination ladder, student demonstrates gross-motor coordination, dynamic balance, body and space awareness and kinesthesis.

EQUIPMENT
Jump box with incline board, coordination ladder and mats.

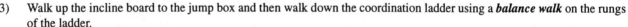

CHALLENGES
1) Perform a *balance walk* on the rungs of the coordination ladder until you reach the top of the jump box and then walk down the incline board.

2) Perform a four-legged *dog walk* on the sides or rungs of the coordination ladder until you reach the top of the jump box and then move down the incline board using a four-legged *dog walk* again. (For *dog walk*: Lesson 1, Station 2, 3rd Week, *Mat Stunts*.)

3) Walk up the incline board to the jump box and then walk down the coordination ladder using a *balance walk* on the rungs of the ladder.

4) Walk up the incline board using a *four-legged walk* to the jump box and then move down the coordination ladder using a *four-legged walk*.

5) (If time allows, have the students do this one.) *Creep* up the incline board on your hands and knees to the jump box and then perform a *crab walk* down the coordination ladder. (For *creep*, see Lesson 1, Station 1, 1st Week, "Mat Stunts.") (For *crab walk*, see Lesson 1, Station 2, 16th Week, *Mat Stunts*.) (The *crab walk* down the coordination ladder can be very difficult. Be sure to spot it closely!)

STRESS: Slow controlled movements. Eyes carefully guide all movements.

OVERVIEW OF BASIC PERCEPTUAL-MOTOR EQUIPMENT #1

Hoop

Geometric Shapes

Scooter Board

Jump Standard

Cross Bar

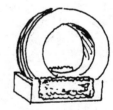

Auto Tire in Support Stand

OVERVIEW OF BASIC PERCEPTUAL-MOTOR EQUIPMENT #2

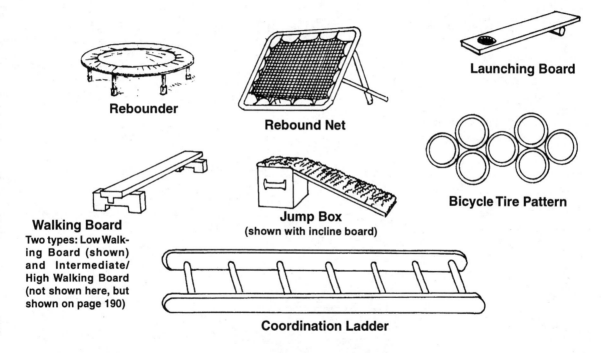

Rebounder

Rebound Net

Launching Board

Bicycle Tire Pattern

Walking Board
Two types: Low Walking Board (shown) and Intermediate/ High Walking Board (not shown here, but shown on page 190)

Jump Box
(shown with incline board)

Coordination Ladder

EQUIPMENT CONSTRUCTION DIAGRAMS #1

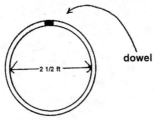

Hoop

Use plastic pipe or tube 8ft long with a 3/4" diameter.
Wood dowel is inserted to help hold hoop together.

dowel

2 1/2 ft

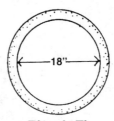

Bicycle Tire

18"

You can also simulate hoops or bicycle tires to jump, run, hop, or step into by arranging 8 **StickySticks™** in an octagon patterrn as shown below.

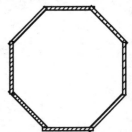

Auto Tire in Support Stand

carpet in box

Auto Tire Support Stand

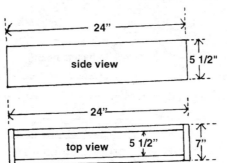

24"

side view

5 1/2"

24"

top view   5 1/2"   7"

7"

end view   5 1/2"

EQUIPMENT CONSTRUCTION DIAGRAMS #2

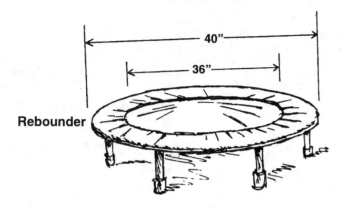

Rebounder

40"

36"

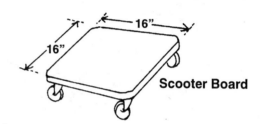

Scooter Board

16"

16"

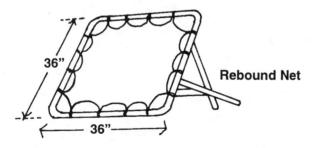

Rebound Net

36"

36"

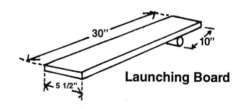

Launching Board

30"

10"

5 1/2"

Level-1 Lessons --- *Page 187* --- *25 Week Program*
Copyright © Jack Capon 1998

EQUIPMENT CONSTRUCTION DIAGRAMS #3

Coordination Ladder (wood version)

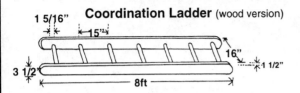

1 5/16"
15"
16"
1 1/2"
3 1/2"
8ft

Coordination Ladder (plastic foam board version)

Made from *Foam Coordination Boards™* Each plastic foam board is 16" long x 5" wide x 2" thick with sticky sides that stick solidly together to form the various lengths (low balance beams can also be made with these foam boards!). A foam board ladder equivalent to the wood one would consist of two 8ft long side rails of 6 boards each plus 5 rungs 15" apart for a total of 17 *Foam Coordination Boards™*

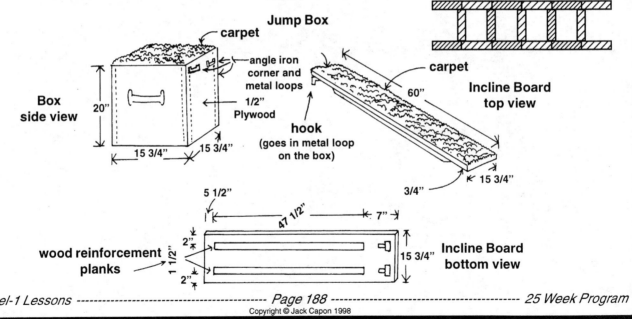

Jump Box

carpet

angle iron corner and metal loops

1/2" Plywood

Box side view

20"

15 3/4"   15 3/4"

hook
(goes in metal loop on the box)

carpet

60"

Incline Board top view

3/4"

15 3/4"

Incline Board bottom view

5 1/2"

47 1/2"   7"

2"
1 1/2"
2"

15 3/4"

wood reinforcement planks

EQUIPMENT CONSTRUCTION DIAGRAMS #4

Geometric Shapes

Shapes can be cut from a 4 foot x 8 foot sheet of plywood 1/2 inch thick. And a second proportionately larger circle, square, rectangle, and triangle can be cut from a separate piece of plywood.

Shapes can also be made from **StickySticks™** which are plastic foam sticks that have velcro® -like sticky sides and ends. These sticks are each 16" long x 2" wide x 2" thick. They easily and solidly stick together to form all the crawl-through geometric shapes and other equipment items as well. The beauty of **StickySticks™** is, of course, that they are not only very lightweight and extremely safe and friendly to work with, but that they can be easily taken apart and reconfigured into other shapes and at the end of the day can be taken apart once again to be stored compactly away and out of sight.

This circle or octagon
takes 12 **StickySticks™**

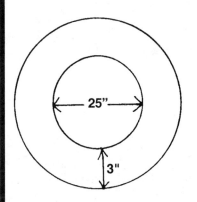

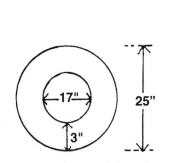

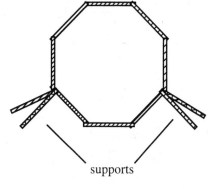

supports

EQUIPMENT CONSTRUCTION DIAGRAMS #5

Large Square

25"

31"

3"

Geometric Shape Support Stand (solid or laminated wood)

1/2"

5"

15"

Small Square

25"

20"

3"

Small Square = 10
Large = 14
StickySticks™

Geometric Shapes (continued)

more plans for shapes made out of plywood and *StickySticks™*

Small Rectangle = 8
Large = 12
StickySticks™

Large Rectangle

20"

30"

36"

3"

26"

Large Triangle

33"

19 1/2"

3"

Small Rectangle

30"

12"

22"

3"

Small Triangle = 8
Large = 11
StickySticks™

EQUIPMENT CONSTRUCTION DIAGRAMS #6

Intermediate/High Walking Board

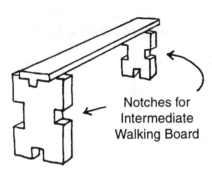

Notches for Intermediate Walking Board

Note that the notches for the Intermediate Walking Board are on both sides and the notches for the High Walking Board are on the top and bottom. The different size notches allow for either the wide or narrow side of the walking board, depending on the walking experience desired. Simply flip the walking board supports over to create an Intermediate Walking Board or a High Walking Board.

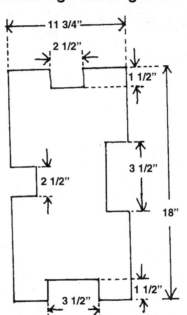

Combination Intermediate/High Walking Board Supports

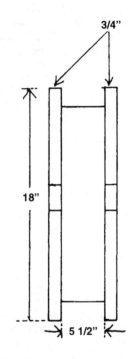

EQUIPMENT CONSTRUCTION DIAGRAMS #7

Low Walking Board
(plastic foam board version)

= 10 boards

= 8 boards

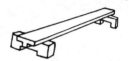

Low Walking Board
(wood version)

Made from *Foam Coordination Boards™* Each
plastic foam board is 16" long x 5" wide x 2" thick (or 2" off the ground) with sticky sides that stick
solidly together to form various lengths. Also, other walking board configurations can be made,
like a zig-zag walking board, a walking board tree, and so on. To form a straight walking board
like the one shown above, it takes 5 foam boards for a 6ft 8" board, 6 foam boards for an 8ft
board, and 8 foam boards for a 10ft 8" long board. When you're done, boards can be easily taken
apart to make other configurations or compactly stored away.

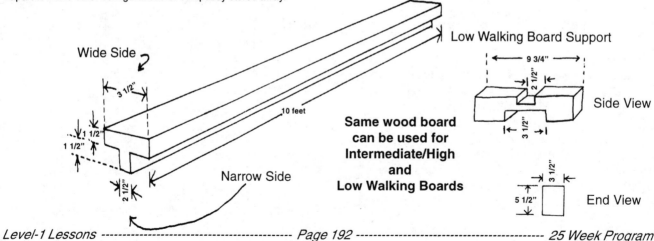

Wide Side

3 1/2"

1 1/2"

1 1/2"

2 1/2"

10 feet

Narrow Side

**Same wood board
can be used for
Intermediate/High
and
Low Walking Boards**

Low Walking Board Support

9 3/4"

2 1/2"

3 1/2"

3 1/2"

Side View

3 1/2"

5 1/2"

End View

EQUIPMENT CONSTRUCTION DIAGRAMS #8

Cross Bar Assembled

Game Cone

Cross Bars and Game Cones

hole

weight

Cross Tube end with
knotted cord and weight

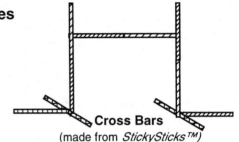

Cross Bars
(made from Game Cones, plastic tubes and rope)

This type of cross bar can be easily assembled by combining two game cones and a plastic cross tube (plastic tubes that golf clubs fit into when sold in stores or thin walled, flexible but rigid, plastic pipe or tubing). The plastic cross tubes are three feet in length. The cross tube is held to the cones by small knotted ropes or cords. The cords are attached to the tube and hang down loose inside of the cones. Weights, which are attached to the ends of the cords inside of the cones, hold the cross tube in place. The height of the cross tube is easily adjusted since the attached weighted ropes are knotted (to catch on the cone's edge) and hang free inside of the cones. (Note: cross bars are interchangeable with jump standards and both serve the same purpose of providing an obstacle to go over or under.)

Cross Bars
(made from *StickySticks™*)

By using *StickySticks™* as shown above, you can make a cross bar or jump standard whose bar height can be infinitely varied either higher or lower. The example shown above is made from 10 sticks.

Game Cones (foam stick version)

Can be your traditional plastic cones or easily simulated by 2 *StickySticks™* as shown below.

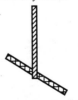

Game Cones (plastic cone version)

Cones are not only used in constructing cross bars, but also serve as useful obstacles by themselves. Plastic cones which have holes in their tops and are about 18 inches high make the best components of cross bars made from game cones.

Ropes

Get 100 to 200 foot coils of 3/8 inch cotton sash cord or rope. (Polyethelene cords are also suitable.) Cut the cord into 7 or 8 foot lengths. Tape, knot, or melt (in the case of polyethelene cords) the ends to prevent unraveling.

Bean Bags

Bean bags can be easily made. Just use a durable fabric like sailcloth, denim, burlap, light canvas, etc., and.....

1) Cut the material into 8" x 4" rectangles.
2) Fold the 8" side in half.
3) On the sewing machine, using a short stitch length and swing 1/4" from the outer edges, sew along two sides. Leave the third side open so the bag can be turned inside out to hide the stitching and be filled.
4) After turning the bag inside out, sue a pinking shear, and pink along the open edges of the bag.
5) Fill the bag three quarters full with either rice, small beans, or clean aquarium gravel.
6) Use two extra long paper clips or bobby pins to hold filling in while sewing a row of stitches 1/2" from the pinked edge.
7) If you like, for reinforcement, sew a second row of stitches 3/8" from the pinked edge.

EQUIPMENT CONSTRUCTION DIAGRAMS #9

Jump Standard with cross bar placed over the top of the loops

JUMP STANDARD
(wood version)

Poles

Cross Bar

3ft 6 1/2"

Pole dimensions

1 5/16"

6/8"

4 ft

Cross Bar dimensions

1 5/8"   7 1/2"

7 1/2"

7/8"

Base Support dimensions

JUMP STANDARD
(foam stick version)

A Jump Standard can also be solidly made from 10 *StickyStics™* as shown above. However, in contrast to the wood version, it is completely safe and friendly and can be easily used to construct other safe and friendly equipment items, geometric shapes and obstacles and then be disassembled and compactly put away at the end of the day!

1 3/8"

6/8"

2"

8"

Loop dimensions

Loop folded in half and riveted together

rivets

Loop mounted on one of the poles

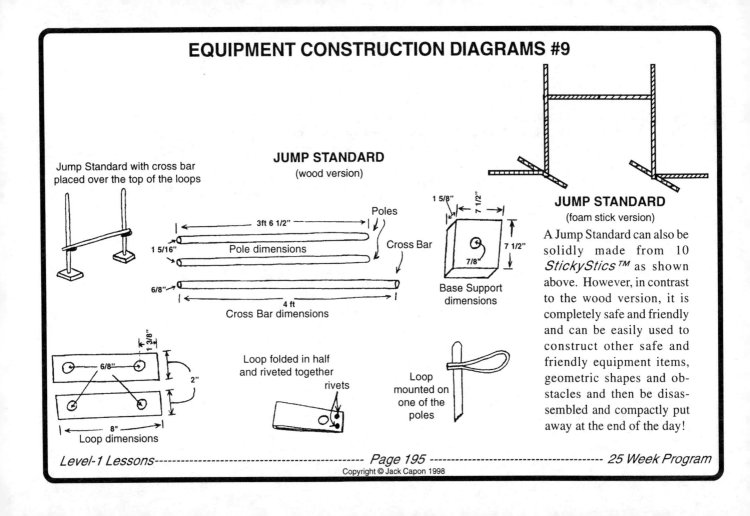

Jump Standards (wood version)

Jump Standards can be easily made by using the plans on the previous page. Height of Jump Standard is readily adjusted by sliding the tight fitting loops up and down the poles. Loops are either made from leather or rubber tire strips that are at least 1/8" thick. Poles should fit tightly in the base supports and can even be glued in place. A cross bar can be laid across the tops of the loops, as shown on the previous page, for easy removal or slipped through the loops. For safety considerations the cross bar should be placed across the tops of the loops so that a child will not trip over it or bring down both poles and the cross bar when the child can't quite make it over the cross bar. Only the cross bar should come down when a child hits it.

Some Thoughts On Equipment Construction

Most of the perceptual-motor equipment in this curriculum guide is relatively simple to construct. Equipment construction for the wood equipment items would make an excellent project for junior-high and senior-high school wood and metal shops. It would not only be inexpensive, but would provide a valuable learning experience. Wood equipment could be literally "made to order" for your particular perceptual-motor needs.

Another possibility is a local carpenter, parent with carpentry skills or lumber yard and/or local metal shop. This would give business to your local area, help in generating community support, and, in many cases, be less expensive. As in the case of school district wood shop and metal shop classes, you would be able to work closely with them and get a "tailor made" product. Many large equipment manufacturers started out in someone's garage making products for local schools and institutions.

Some other ideas that come to mind are organizations such as the Goodwill and handicapped centers, etc. They are ready, willing and able to make good quality equipment items to your specifications at somewhat above cost. When you give them your business, you not only get quality equipment made to the exact specifications for your situation, but you are also helping them.

And then, of course, equipment items that can be made from **Foam Coordination Boards**™ *or* **StickySticks**™ *can be easily constructed with great enthusiasm by the students themselves and in this way tranforms the equipment set-up activity as yet another skill-building challenge in your perceptual-motor program.*

Program Suppliers

The publisher, Front Row Experience, and many educational stores in the United States, Canada, and Australia sell the printed components of Jack Capon's Perceptual-Motor Program, Levels 1 and 2. Equivalent equipment components of Jack's Program can be found in most sports equipment stores and some educational stores. Although most equipment items will be found to vary from the exact specifications called for, they will be near enough so that they can be easily adapted to the Program. The publisher also sells some equipment items. For a free catalog on all the products sold by the publisher, visit the world-wide web at : **www.frontrowexperience.com** or phone or fax toll-free **800-524-9091** or phone or fax **925-634-5710**.

Program Equipment List

The following equipment list shows the types of equipment needed and how many of each. Most of the equipment listed here was illustrated in the Overview Of Basic Perceptual-Motor Equipment and in the Equipment Construction Diagrams sections.

The individual cost of equipment items is not given because of constant price fluctuations. However, of the total equipment cost, you'll find nearly half of it is borne by the "tumbling mats." If your school already has mats, then you will save quite a bit. Any other similar equipment items you already have will save you still more. Your school or district may be able to make some equipment inexpensively. Also, some items such as bowling pins, bicycle and car tires can many times be obtained free (in worn or damaged condition, but usable) from bowling alleys, bike and car repair shops, etc.

Equipment Needed	Quantity	Equipment Needed	Quantity
Low Walking Board (7" off the ground)	1	Combination Intermediate/High Board (11" to 20 1/2" off the ground)	1

Equipment Needed	Quantity	Equipment Needed	Quantity
Coordination Ladder (8ft long)	1	Game Cones (18" high)	6
Rebounder (jogging exerciser) 40" diameter frame, 8" high	1	Plastic Cross Tubes with weighted cord	3
Geometric Shapes (8 shapes of 2 circles, 2 squares, 2 rectangles and 2 triangles)	1 set	Jump Box with Incline Board (20" high x 15 3/4" wide)	1
Tire Support Stand (24" long x 7" wide)	1	Scooter Board (large 16" x 16"	1
Ropes (7ft long, 3/8" to 1/2" diameter)	6	Jump Standards (optional, can be used in place of Cross Bars on Game Cones)	3
Tracking Ball (small tennis ball-like on a cord)	1	Bicycle Tires (used, standard size)	12
Bowling Pins (used and damaged)	2	Bean Bags (set of 12 oblong bags made to fit in the palm of the hand)	1 set
Auto Tire (used, standard size)	1	Rubber Balls (7" in diameter)	4

Equipment Needed	Quantity	Equipment Needed	Quantity
Plastic Hoops (30" in diameter)	12	Tumbling Mats (2" thick, 4ft x 6ft)	6
Launching Board	1	Rebound Net (36" x 36" or larger)	1

Parent Communication Aides

In the following section we are offering you a variety of Parent Communication Aides that schools have found extremely helpful in implementing the Capon Perceptual-Motor Program. If you feel any of these aides would be helpful in your situation, please feel free to use or modify them for your own use. Part of the success of implementing the Capon Perceptual-Motor Program is directly related to good communication with parents.

— Special Message To Parents —

Often in our rush to give children a head start in pursuit of academic excellence we, as parents, overlook a vital part of the child's development. The motor system forms a foundation for the growth and expansion of all human organisms. It must be carefully nurtured.

Why Is Perceptual-Motor Development Important To Your Child?

The brain controls the muscles of the body and the ability of the brain to send the proper signals to these muscles depends upon, among other things, previous experiences. Walking, eye movement, balancing, throwing, writing and doing somersaults are all motor activities that are performed by muscles, dictated by the brain, and dependent upon thousands of previous experiences. Some activities require large muscle coordination, such as jumping rope. Others, such as drawing a square, depend upon fine (small) muscle movement from both eyes and fingers. Much of basic school readiness depends upon many muscles working together. Just standing, for instance, depends on the proper tension and extension of 200 opposing muscles. When one considers the complexity of jumping rope.....the coordination of leg, hand, eye, body and arm muscles.....the precision of muscle control is fantastic!

Body movement of the newborn child starts with random movement of large muscles and by the time he or she enters school, a very complex communication system between brain and muscles must be developed. Each progressive step requires a series of developmental experiences. A child must first stand, then step, then walk, then run. Each milestone is an indicator of previous successes in movement.

Catching and throwing a ball is often too complex an activity for a four year old. He or she must first be able to stop a rolled ball. To do this requires an estimation of its arrival time and bringing the hands together at the right moment. This involves fingers, arms and eyes. The next step might be catching a large size bouncing ball, then a medium size ball thrown directly to the hands and finally a small ball. The eyes must work as a coordinated pair of range finders. One eye is all that is necessary for reading and recognizing objects. Two eyes are necessary to determine distance and arrival time of a thrown object. Later in school, reading will depend in part upon the movement of the eyes across the page. This skill is enhanced by successful experiences in catching a rolled ball earlier in life.

It is important to note that all communication skills.....reading, writing, speech and gesturing are motor based abilities. Children who are deprived of a wide variety of movement experiences, especially through natural play opportunities, run the risk of perceptual and motor impairment. The child who climbs, rides a bicycle, skates, teeters on a balance board, tumbles on the carpet and jumps on the bed has a better chance for good coordination than does the well-behaved child who sits placidly in a chair "minding manners" or watching television.

Movement experiences become a vital part of the normal development for all children. We cannot afford to leave motor development to "chance."

Activities To Help Your Child Develop Basic Perceptual-Motor Abilities At Home

The activities that follow are examples of experiences which you can encourage or guide your child into within your normal home environment. Not only should you provide equipment and/or materials for purposeful movement activities to take place, but, as often as possible, you should participate with your child. The activities have been listed under the basic motor abilities they help the child to refine.

Balance Activities
1) Riding bicycles, scooters, etc.
2) Using stilts, pogo sticks, etc.
3) Roller skating, skate boards, etc.
4) Walking board tasks (use a 2" x 4" board, 8 to 10 feet long).
5) Tumbling stunts on the carpet (forward rolls, head stand, etc.)
6) Jumping on old mattress springs (use like a trampoline).
7) Climbing stairs, small ladders, etc.
8) Challenge your child to balance on various body parts and use different body supports.

Eye-Hand Coordination Activities

1) Ball bouncing and ball catching.
2) Tetherball, punching bag, etc.
3) Rope jumping.
4) Rebound net for throwing and catching.
5) Tapping balloons in the air.
6) Marbles, jacks, etc.
7) Plastic scoops (made out of clorox bottles, drinking water bottles, milk bottles, etc.) used with tennis balls or bean bags.
8) Playing with hoops, frisbees, etc.
9) Ring toss and bean bag throw games.
10) Coloring, painting, drawing, etc.
11) Cutting with scissors.
12) Puzzles, stringing beads, sewing burlap, etc.
13) Hammering nails into boards.
14) Sand box play, clay work, cutting cookies, etc.
15) Playing piano or organ, typing, etc.

Eye-Foot Coordination Activities

1) Jumping rope.
2) Kicking balls.
3) Climbing stairs, ladders, etc.
4) Walking on masking tape lines, ropes, etc.
5) Jumping and hopping into obstacles like old bike tires, hoops, rope in a circle, etc.
6) Hopscotch.

7) Stepping over objects of various heights (boxes, cans, etc.).
8) Stepping on footprint patterns cut from cardboard or craft paper.

Body And Space Awareness Activities
1) Identifying basic body parts.....elbows, shoulders, knees, etc.
2) Drawing pictures of self or friends and identify body parts.
3) Move body parts as challenged: nod head, clap hands, bend elbows, shrug shoulders, etc.
4) Simple obstacle course (going over, under, between, through, into, around objects).
5) Jumping and/or hopping into bicycles tires, hoops, etc.
6) Crawling through play tunnels, boxes, etc.
7) Swinging, climbing, exploring using backyard play equipment.
8) Ask your child to move forward, backward, sideways, etc., without touching nearby objects.

Locomotor (Transport) Activities
1) Moving to music using records.
2) Crawling and/or creeping on the carpet.
3) Rope jumping.
4) Jumping from objects, over obstacles, etc.
5) Hopping and/or jumping into tires, hoops, etc.
6) Skipping, galloping challenges.
7) Running short races, around obstacles, etc.
8) Hopscotch type games.

— Perceptual-Motor Program Announcement To Parents —

As a part of our School District Physical Education Curriculum, perceptual-motor activities are offered to boys and girls in grades Kindergarten through the Third Grade and Special Education Classes. The perceptual-motor activities are conducted indoors and involve the use of approximately twenty equipment items. In this carefully planned program, boys and girls are presented with a wide variety of movement experiences designed to improve physical coordination, enhance basic sensory functioning and promote a positive self image.

For the safety and maximum benefit of participants, it is required that all children remove their shoes and socks before a lesson begins. The clothing that children wear to school on the days that this program is offered is very important to successful, safe and comfortable performance. It is recommended that the girls wear pants to school on the days the program is conducted and that tights *not* be worn on these days. Tights are very slippery and lead to accidents. Long dresses are also especially hazardous.

Your child participates in this Program on _____ . Your cooperation in arranging for proper types of clothing to be worn on the Perceptual-Motor Program days would be greatly appreciated.

— Volunteer Aide Recruitment Letter —

Our School District is presently recruiting volunteer aides from the community to assist Kindergarten through the Third Grade and Special Education teachers in conducting the District Perceptual-Motor Program. The Perceptual-Motor Program is a part of the Physical Education Program and is designed to improve mind and body communication through the use of carefully selected movement experiences. The goals of the Program are: 1) To assist each child in acquiring efficient movement; 2) Improvement of sensory functioning; and 3) Development of a positive self-image.

In order for this program to be fully effective, teachers need aides to help guide and motivate the children while they participate in small group station activities. Volunteer Aides will be asked to give approximately one hour of their time each week. The day and time will be coordinated by the schools and teachers involved. A Training Workshop for volunteer aides will be conducted. The Workshop will cover program rational, organization and use of equipment, teaching techniques and actual demonstrations using children. Attendance at the Training Workshop is most important for assisting in the Program. The Workshop will take place on _____ from 9:00 A.M. to 11:15 A.M. at _____ . Anyone interested in the Program is invited to attend.

If you are able to offer assistance in the Perceptual-Motor Program, please complete the form below.
- -
(Detach here and return to the teacher you wish to assist or to the school office.)

Name: _____ Telephone: _____

School: _____ Grade Level you would like to assist: _____

Check appropriate box below:
- ❑ 1) **Yes**, I would like to assist in the Perceptual-Motor Program and **will** attend the training workshop for Volunteer Aides on _____ from 9:00 A.M. to 11: 15 A.M. at _____ .

- ❑ 2) **Yes**, I would like to assist in the Perceptual-Motor Program, but will not be able to attend the training course.

- ❑ 3) **Yes**, I am interested in assisting with the Perceptual-Motor Program, but I am **not available** at the present time. Please call on me at a later date, if help is needed.

Days available: _____ . Times available: _____ .

— Perception Games —

These Perception Games are offered as supplementary classroom activities to the basic Perceptual-Motor Program. They can be used in the regular classroom and by parents at home to sharpen the students' perceptual abilities in the visual and auditory areas. They are "fun" learning experiences for children which require no special equipment. Listening and memory sequencing skills are enriched through participation in these activities.

Visual Discrimination

1) **What Is Missing?**

   Six to nine objects are arranged in a row on a table or chalkboard ledge, as children watch. Children then cover their eyes. The Teacher removes one or two objects. A child is then asked what has been taken away.

2) **What Is This Shape?**

   The teacher "draws in the air" a large outline of some object in the room. The children are asked to look around and guess what was outlined. Sometimes hints as to the location of the objects are needed. The teacher may also *draw in the air* numbers or letters of the alphabet and call on the children to identify the correct one.

3) **Find a Shape Like This**

   The teacher shows a cardboard circle form. A child is asked to touch everything in sight in the room that is the same shape (or give the child a definite number of objects to touch that are the same shape). The teacher then shows other forms such as a square, rectangle, triangle, etc.

4) **Each In Its Place**

   The teacher or the child arranges three, four or five objects in a row, while the rest of the children cover their eyes. The children look at the objects for several seconds. Then one child is called on to face the class (turning his or her back toward the row of objects) and name them in order, while the other children watch. The order of the objects is then changed.

5) **Hide Away**

Using a brown paper bag (or a large basket), the teacher goes around the classroom holding up objects, then placing them in a bag. One child is chosen to tell what is in the bag; another child takes the objects out. The rest of the class involves itself by giving hints as to what's in the bag. This game will be enjoyed more if the teacher and the children bring a variety of things to put in the bag.

6) **Touch Four People**

The teacher goes around the room, touching four or five people. A child is asked to tell who was touched, giving names in correct order. I the child can't remember, hints are given, such as: "It's someone with red on." A variation of this game would be touching four objects.

7) **Get Something Bigger**

The teacher places a very small object on a table. A number of children are called on, in turn, to get something bigger and place it on the table. It is fun to try to get something larger than the object each time. If rocks are available, it is especially fun.

8) **Get Something Smaller**

The preceding game in reverse.

9) **One From the Ring**

Have the children sit in a circle (ring). Place balls (or another group of objects) of different colors in the center. The children hide their eyes while one child removes one of the balls. The object of the game is to tell which color ball has been removed. The child who is called upon, and knows the correct color, has the next turn. The difficulty of the game is, of course, determined by the number of balls placed in the center.

10) **I Spy**

The teacher describes an object without mentioning its name. The children look around the room until they locate the object which she described. The first one to say, "I Spy," and who correctly identifies the object, has the next turn to describe something in the classroom.

Auditory Discrimination

1) <u>**Who Has The Castanet?**</u>

One child stands in front of the room with his or her back turned to the group. Another child is given the castanet. All the children keep their hands behind their backs and pretend to be shaking the castanet. The child who is the guesser turns and listens for the castanet. He or she then attempts to guess who has the castanet. You may wish to use a bell or other type of noise maker.

2) <u>**Finishing Rhymes**</u>

The teacher repeats a rhyme. The 2nd and 3rd times, the children come in with the last words as the teacher stops. For example: "Hickery Dickery _____ , the mouse ran up the _____ ." Start with familiar ones.

3) <u>**Securing Objects**</u>

The teacher asks, "Who would like to try to get four things that we mention?" She then names, for example, a book, a ball, a top and a piece of paper. A child goes and gets the four things. If there are the "makings" of a grocery store or toy store in the room, the game could be played "doing an errand at the store." Another variation would be to give the names of four people and have a child tap them in the order named.

4)   **Movement Sequences**
The teacher verbally gives movement directions to a child or a class and they attempt to respond in the correct order. For example, the teacher can say> "Take two steps forward, turn around, then clap twice," and so on. This is excellent sequential memory training.

5)   **Telephone Pole**
The teacher gives a series of directions quickly, such as "Clap your hands, hop on all fours, point to the ceiling, jump, stamp your feet." When the teacher calls, "Telephone Pole," all the children straighten up and stand still like "telephone poles."

6)   **Tap The Rhythm**
The teacher taps a rhythmic beat. One child, then the whole group, copies the beat. Rhythm sticks or pencils may be used, or the children may clap the rhythm.

7)   **Who Is It?**
A child in the class is described. Others try to guess who has been described.

8)   **Name The Animal**
The teacher places pictures of about eight animals in plain view. Then she or he describes one without naming it. A child is asked to come up and touch the animal described. (Or the teacher may read a rhyme about an animal without naming it.) A good variation would be to let one child give the description. The game can be played with pictures of

foods, homes, means of transportation, workers, tools, etc. Objects could be used instead of pictures.

9) **Let's Act It**

The teacher tells a short story. Whenever there is action or facial expression indicated, the teacher says, "Let's all show what he did," or "Let's show how she looked."

10) **What Song Am I Tapping?**

The teacher may mention the names of three familiar songs. The teacher then taps the rhythm of several bars of one of the songs mentioned. The children try to guess which song it was.

11) **What Did I Tap?**

The teacher goes around the room slowly, tapping each of six or seven objects with a tom tom beater. (Objects would be of wood, metal, glass and cardboard.) Then the children cover their eyes. The teacher taps each one 3 times. A child is asked to identify one at a time by telling what type of object....cardboard, metal, etc...., or by tapping the object. If he or she is correct, another object is tried.

12) **High, Low, Or In Between**

The children cover their eyes. The teacher taps something up high. The children uncover their eyes and try to guess whether the object was high, low, or "in between." If just one child at a time is the guesser, the game goes better than having the whole class call out.

13) **Hide The Spool**

Once child is sent from the room. When another has hidden a spool or other object, a doorkeeper invites the child to reenter the room. The others indicate to the child where the object is by clapping their hands. If he or she approaches the object, they clap softly, and if he or she goes away from the object they begin clapping louder. If a child locates the object, he or she has the next turn to hide it.

14) **<u>Listen And Do</u>**

At first, the children imitate the actions of the teacher who may put her hands on her head, shoulders, knees, behind her back, etc. Then the teacher says one thing, but does another. The children must follow the directions of her spoken words rather than imitate the actions. (This is similar to "Simon Says.")

Lessons Grouped According to Equipment and Type of Activities

Organizing your activities around equipment or types of activities may help your program run more smoothly. If all classes in the program use activities involving only certain types of equipment, then everyone can share in the use of the equipment on that particulur day.

When classroom space is lacking for storage and use of the equipment, many schools use wood storage sheds on the playground or nearby to house the equipment. When equipment is stored in this manner, the activities are usually performed right on the playground. (Don't forget to use mats around the equipment for safety and for doing many of the activities on. This is so even when rubberized pavement to play on is available.) And when all classes in the program are coordinated in using the same kinds of equipment for various activities, they can all share in the set-up, use, and take-down of equipment common to all of the different activities they are doing. Naturally, when perfoming the activities in a coordinated manner on the playground, some modifications have to made. For example, the program calls for kids to be in their bare feet for increased tactile awareness. However, it may take too much time taking shoes and socks off and putting them on again plus various areas of the playground may not be too friendly to bare feet. And other modifications may be necessary.

This equipment/activity coordinated method of doing the program right on the playground with equipment stored there has been very successful for schools in the Los Angeles Unified School District in California. Since there is an acute shortage of class-room space and classes are on a year-round schedule, this method makes the best sense for them in their situation. When equipment is stored outside on the playground you might think that there would be more of a problem of pilferage, vandalism, etc. But experience over the years has shown that there are more problems of this nature right in the classroom than in the storage sheds. In fact, no perceptual-motor equipment property has been stolen to date from the sheds over a 10 to 15 year period. The same can't be said of the classrooms, however.

There are other reasons to group the activities. In order to integrate the Level-1 Program with traditional P.E., you might want to consider using the Ball activities as a lead-up or a warm-up for P.E. activities that involve the use of balls. The pairing of other

Level-1 activities with sports/games that depend on the skills developed and reinforced by certain Level-1 lessons would go a long way toward toward the total development of the child and the acceptance of Jack Capon's program at your school.

Coordination Ladder = Page #'s 39, 45, 57, 63, 81, 97, 108, 122, 132, 145, 157, 163, 170, 175, 183.

Mat Stunts = Page #'s 36, 43, 49, 55, 61, 67, 73, 79, 85, 94, 100, 106, 112, 118, 124, 131, 137, 143, 149, 155, 161, 167, 173, 179.

Pattern Activities = Page #'s 41, 50, 53, 62, 70, 74, 80, 107, 110, 119, 125, 138, 150, 156, 162, 174, 180, 182.

Jump Box = Page #'s 52, 59, 68, 76, 88, 95, 113, 126, 135, 144, 151, 159, 163, 175, 183.

Rebound Net & Launching Board = Page #'s 65, 77, 86, 98, 104, 116, 129, 171.

Obstacle Courses (includes Pattern Activities) = Page #'s 40, 41, 46, 50, 53, 56, 58, 62, 64, 70, 74, 80, 82, 103, 107, 110, 119, 125, 138, 150, 156, 162, 168, 174, 180, 182.

Geometric Shapes = Page #'s 47, 51, 69, 75, 87, 96, 114.

Low & Intermediate/High Walking Boards = Page #'s 42, 48, 54, 60, 66, 72, 78, 84, 93, 99, 105, 111, 117, 123, 130, 136, 142, 148, 154, 160, 166, 172, 178.

Scooter Board = Page #'s 120, 128, 139, 152, 158, 164, 176.

Rebounder = Page #'s 102, 109, 115, 121, 133, 140, 146, 153, 165, 169, 177, 181.

Ball Skills = Page #'s 44, 56, 71, 83, 101, 108, 114, 122, 127, 130, 134, 136, 141, 142, 148, 159, 172, 178, 179, 181, 182.

Bean Bags = Page #'s 38, 60, 65, 77, 78, 86, 87, 98, 104, 110, 116, 123, 129, 130, 170, 171.

Hoops or Bike Tires = Page #'s 38, 41, 50, 53, 56, 59, 62, 66, 68, 70, 74, 76, 80, 82, 88, 93, 103, 107, 110, 113, 119, 125, 127, 134, 135, 136, 138, 141, 148, 150, 151, 154, 156, 162, 163, 168, 174, 175, 180, 182.

Ropes = Page #'s 37, 53, 74, 84, 107, 125, 134, 150, 152, 156, 162, 174, 175, 180.

Jump Standards or Cross Bars mounted on Cones = Page #'s 40, 46, 48, 50, 58, 64, 66, 70, 80, 82, 88, 93, 103, 119, 125, 136, 138, 139, 147, 151, 162, 168, 176.

Cones Alone (without Cross Tubes) = Page #'s 71, 89, 101, 128, 158, 164.

Car Tire in Support Stand = Page #'s 46, 58, 64, 82, 103, 168.

Resources

The following people would be happy to help you start, restart, or continue Jack Capon's Movement Education programs for your school. You will need to contact them directly and make arrangements with them for any assistance in an advisory capacity or in conducting workshops, in-service training, etc. for the teachers, parents, and administrators at your school or District. Any fees, stipends, honorariums and/or transportation and lodging costs will have to be worked out with them. Let them know that you were referred to them by their voluntary listing in the back of Jack Capon's Level-1 book.

John King
4013 Godrey Drive
Salida, CA 95368
Phone: 1-209-545-2619

Eleni K. Wanken
Mountain Blvd. Preschool Learning Center
4432 Mountain Blvd.
Oakland, CA 94619
Phone: 1-925-838-7434

Ursula Jasinski de Hernandez
9055 Martindale Ave
Latuna Canyon, CA 91352
Phone: 1-818-768-7202
E-Mail = LUA1@aol.com

Deborah Opperud
Elementary P.E. Specialist
Educational Services Dept.
Alameda Unified School District
2200 Central Ave
Alameda, CA 94501
Phone: 1-510-337-7063

FREE
PUBLISHER'S CATALOG

on the world-wide web or in your hands!

Includes more Movement Coordination Lesson Plans, Movement Coordination Equipment used in the Level-1 program and beyond, and fine-motor/gross-motor coordination kits!

See an up-to-the-minute catalog at:
www.frontrowexperience.com

or put one in your hands by Phoning or Faxing either of the two numbers below:
Toll-Free: 800-524-9091 or 925-634-5710

or by writing to:
FRONT ROW EXPERIENCE
540 Discovery Bay Blvd.
Discovery Bay, CA 94514-9454, United States of America